A Prototype and Anger i...

This innovative book applies findings from the field of cognitive linguistics to the study of emotions in the Hebrew Bible. The book draws on the prototype approach to conceptual categories to help interpret emotion language in biblical passages. Contemporary scholarship has come to recognize that biblical emotion terms do not necessarily possess exact equivalents within our modern lexicons, even if some of these terms express (or appear to express) concepts similar to those conveyed by modern emotion language. In particular, the book focuses on *sn'* and *ḥrh*, which are almost always equated in modern English with *hate* and *anger*. However, the ancient Hebrew roots evoke varied and robust emotion-scripts that are quite different than their English counterparts. We see how the prototype script model may help to expose the unique nuances of *sn'* and *ḥrh* and put into profile elements of these emotions that may otherwise go unnoticed. Overall, the study demonstrates that even though modern emotion terms cannot fully capture the ancient emotional experience, our shared use of language to evoke meaning offers us entrée into the emotional world represented in the Hebrew Bible.

Deena E. Grant is Associate Professor of Jewish Studies at Hartford International University for Religion and Peace, USA.

Routledge Interdisciplinary Perspectives on Biblical Criticism

Cain, Abel, and the Politics of God
An Agambenian reading of Genesis 4:1-16
Julián Andrés González Holguín

Epistemology and Biblical Theology
From the Pentateuch to Mark's Gospel
Dru Johnson

Thinking Sex with the Great Whore
Deviant Sexualities and Empire in the Book of Revelation
Luis Menéndez-Antuña

A Philosophical Theology of the Old Testament
A historical, experimental, comparative and analytic perspective
Jaco Gericke

Human Agency and Divine Will
The Book of Genesis
Charlotte Katzoff

Paul and Diversity
A New Perspective on Σάρξ and Resilience in Galatians
Linda Joelsson

A Prototype Approach to Hate and Anger in the Hebrew Bible
Conceiving Emotions
Deena Grant

https://www.routledge.com/Routledge-Interdisciplinary-Perspectives-on-Biblical-Criticism/book-series/RIPBC

A Prototype Approach to Hate and Anger in the Hebrew Bible
Conceiving Emotions

Deena E. Grant

Routledge
Taylor & Francis Group
LONDON AND NEW YORK

First published 2023
by Routledge
4 Park Square, Milton Park, Abingdon, Oxon OX14 4RN

and by Routledge
605 Third Avenue, New York, NY 10158

Routledge is an imprint of the Taylor & Francis Group, an informa business

© 2023 Deena E. Grant

The right of Deena E. Grant to be identified as author of this work has been asserted in accordance with sections 77 and 78 of the Copyright, Designs and Patents Act 1988.

All rights reserved. No part of this book may be reprinted or reproduced or utilised in any form or by any electronic, mechanical, or other means, now known or hereafter invented, including photocopying and recording, or in any information storage or retrieval system, without permission in writing from the publishers.

Trademark notice: Product or corporate names may be trademarks or registered trademarks, and are used only for identification and explanation without intent to infringe.

British Library Cataloguing-in-Publication Data
A catalogue record for this book is available from the British Library

ISBN: 978-1-032-35655-6 (hbk)
ISBN: 978-1-032-39172-4 (pbk)
ISBN: 978-1-003-34871-9 (ebk)

DOI: 10.4324/9781003348719

Typeset in Sabon
by KnowledgeWorks Global Ltd.

Contents

1 Introduction   1

2 Discerning Modern Hate and Anger Scripts   14

3 Broad Biblical *Sn'*-Script   28

4 Narrative *Sn'*-Scripts   33

5 Poetic and Prophetic *Sn'*-Scripts   47

6 Broad Biblical *Ḥrh*-Script   62

7 Narrative *Ḥrh*-Scripts   68

8 Divine *Ḥrh*-Scripts in Old Poetry and in the Prophets   81

9 Conclusion   91

Bibliography   *95*
Index   *102*

1 Introduction

Emotions through a Cross-Cultural Lens

Are emotions a common universal experience or are they socially constructed? The question has motivated a great deal of debate over the years. Charles Darwin argued for the former. Viewing emotions as physiological changes, Darwin believed that emotional expressions evolved, along with other physical traits, through adaptive evolution. Conscious physical changes, like the baring of teeth when angry, as well as autonomic physiological changes, like the hair on one's arm standing on end in fright, occur because at one point in time they held an evolutionary advantage.[1]

Darwin's view finds support, perhaps most famously, in Paul Ekman's work on facial expressions across cultures. Ekman found that members of a remote, preliterate culture reliably linked the same facial expressions to the same emotions as did American subjects. Ekman concluded, from this that facial expressions are pan-cultural and may even represent universal emotions. As Darwin might have explained it, emotions evolved alongside the countenances that now convey them.[2]

While Ekman is right to point out that our common physiology may result in a shared experience of the world, elements of his work are hotly contested. Some argue that even if facial expressions are universal, the emotional experiences that they relay may not be. Others point out that different people experience diverse emotions in response to similar triggers. Dogs provoke fear in some people but elicit affection in others. Is fear of dogs innate, and is affection learned? Is it the converse?[3]

The cognitive psychologist Richard Lazarus argues that emotion differences are driven primarily by individuals' unique interpretations of their encounters. This would explain why, for example, two students might have very different emotional responses to receiving a B+ in an assignment. A student who received only Cs up to that point may appraise B+ as a confirmation of his effort and feel happy. By contrast, a student who received only As up to then may appraise the grade as a rejection of

DOI: 10.4324/9781003348719-1

2 *Introduction*

her effort and feel angry. As cognitive theorists understand it, students experience vastly different emotions because their encounters with the same grade affect their egos in diverse ways.[4]

Once the importance of cognition to the formation of emotions is appreciated, the relevance of what inspires diverse cognitions can be recognized as well. Factors include individual temperament and personal experiences, and also collective culture. Emphasizing the latter, Catherine Lutz describes emotions as "social constructions" that emerge from and guide how diverse societies evaluate the world. Lutz explains:

> The pragmatic and associative networks of meaning in which each emotion word is embedded are extremely rich ones. The complex meaning of each word is the result of the important role those words play in articulating the full range of people's cultural values, social relations, and economic circumstances. Talk about emotions is simultaneously talk about society—about power and politics, about kinship and marriage, about normality and deviance.[5]

According to the cross-cultural linguist Anna Wierzbicka, the terms that different cultures use to denote emotions are portals through which we can discern cross-cultural emotion differences:

> The emotional lexicons of different languages vary considerably, and this points to the profound differences in ideas and beliefs about emotions and between cultural models of emotions .... [I]f people raised in different cultures or sub-cultures come to internalize different ways of describing their experience, this may make what they experience different.[6]

If emotions are, even in part, culturally determined, we cannot assume that an emotion term in the modern English lexicon possesses an exact equivalent within the lexicon of another language. While some emotion terms may translate well into several languages, others may not. Even in cases where English and non-English terms express (or appear to express) similar concepts, they may have any number of differences.

Consider the Thai term *gren jai*, which describes the feeling of being hesitant to accept an offer of help because of the trouble it might cause the person who is offering the help. While this emotion may be felt by Westerners, modern English does not have one term whose semantic range describes this specific scope of experience.[7]

Differences such as this have led some researchers to conclude that "the bulk of mankind lives within systems of thought and feeling that bear little but superficial resemblances to one another."[8] Wierzbicka even suggests that had Ekman exposed his preliterate subjects to emotion terms from a different source language (not English), he would have *discovered* a different set of universal emotions that correspond to the experiences hypercognized in that specific culture:

> I experience a certain unease when reading claims of this kind. ... How is it that these emotions are all so neatly identified by means of English words? For example, Polish does not have a word exactly corresponding to the English word *disgust*. What if psychologists working on the "fundamental emotions" happened to be native speakers of Polish rather than English?[9]

Wierzbicka may be overstating the point. Ekman's work compellingly suggests that, at the very least, some elements of the emotional experience *are* universal. Most likely, emotions are formed from an interaction of distinctive culture *with* universal biology. In this vein, Wierzbicka summarizes: "Emotions are not merely individual sensations or biophysical responses to external stimuli but are mediated by cognitive processes embedded in a particular culture."[10]

In short, the modern study of emotion, which initially sought to determine *whether* emotions are universal or socially constructed, has evolved to study on *how* biology and culture interact to produce emotions. Wierzbicka explains:

> Clearly the ways of thinking and talking about feelings in different cultures and societies (and also in different epochs) exhibit considerable diversity; but neither can there be any doubt about the existence of commonalities and indeed universals.[11]

The problem, she continues, "is how to sort out the cultural-specific from the universal; how to comprehend the former through the latter."[12]

Prototypes

The prototype approach to conceptual categories offers a way to "sort out the cultural-specific from the universal." Prior to the end of the twentieth century, classical theorists had claimed that categories are formed of necessary and sufficient features. As such, emotion categories can be discerned by identifying the traits essential to an emotion concept.[13] By the end of the twentieth century, prototype theorists countered that emotion concepts—conceptual categories, more broadly, for that matter—do not have any essential traits. Encounters are evaluated and instances of an emotion are recognized based on resemblances to a *best* mental representation—a prototype.

4 *Introduction*

I will explain this using the example of the term *bachelor*. The conceptual category BACHELOR possesses two necessary traits: being a man and being unmarried. This means that while a bachelor is necessarily a man and is necessarily unmarried, neither being a man nor being unmarried is sufficient on its own to define a bachelor. Yet, were membership in the category BACHELOR based on necessary and sufficient traits alone, the following question would strike us as unreasonable: Who is a better example of a bachelor, a bartender, or the pope?

How could there be a better or a worse example of a bachelor? Someone either *is* or *is not* a bachelor. The question does make sense to us, though, because membership in a conceptual category exists on a spectrum, with some category members resembling an idealized model more closely than others. Technically, a bartender and the pope are both bachelors—they both possess the traits necessary for membership in this category. The bartender may be perceived as a *better* example of a bachelor because he may resemble the prototype of a BACHELOR more so than the pope.[14]

Where do category prototypes come from? They are formed, at least in part, by experiences. To offer another example, both a dining-room chair and a tatami chair are members of the conceptual category CHAIR. However, an American, who frequently experiences seats as having four legs and a back, may perceive a dining-room chair as a more prototypical member of the category CHAIR, whereas an individual who lives in Japan may perceive a tatami chair as equally or even more "chair-ish."[15]

Emotion-Scripts

Emotion concepts are conceived around culturally distinct prototypes as well. Somewhat differently, though, the traits that form "best examples" of emotions—antecedents, appraisals, physiological reactions, facial expressions, behavioral responses, and the like—are organized sequentially in much the same way as a playwright's script.[16] This means that to know the meanings of category labels like happiness, fear, or jealousy is to know the traits that evoke their scripts.[17] As such, whether a potential instance of an emotion gains membership in a particular emotion category depends on how closely the collection of traits that comprise the instance resembles a prototypical script. A collection may share *many* traits with a particular emotion-script, or it may share only a few especially *salient* ones. Either way, it need not possess any defining traits.[18]

One way that prototype researchers work to unpack the emotion-scripts in a particular culture is by interviewing native speakers. These researchers tend to refrain from asking binary questions such as "Is this or is this not a case of hate?" framing their questions, instead, in terms of degrees of resemblance to a prototype. In this vein, they may ask, "*How good* an example of hate is this scenario?" and "*On a scale* of 1–5, could you rate each word on the basis of *how well* it exemplifies hate?"[19]

Answers to such questions reveal the traits that form an emotion-script, as well as how central each trait is to the script. The relative centrality of traits is especially important because two cultures may share similar emotion-scripts but emphasize different traits therein. For example, Japanese *on* is similar to English "shame," yet intense feelings and committed behaviors are more central and salient to the concept of *on* than they are to the concept of shame:

> [T]he Japanese *on* is all-dominating. It involves a mixture of "love" and "respect," also implying duty and being indebted to someone: from newborn babies who are forever in debt to their parents, to kamikaze pilots for whom the last cigarette given to them just before their final flight reminded them of their permanent indebtedness to the Emperor. Love, kindness, generosity, which we value just in proportion as they are given without strings attached, necessarily must have strings in Japan.[20]

Interviews of native English-speakers about the meaning of the term "hate" find that a perceived offense, a feeling of humiliation, an urge to avoid, and an impulse to harm are central to a prototypical hate-script. Similar interviews about the meaning of the term "anger" find that a perceived offense, an attempt at control, and a loss of control are central to a prototypical anger-script. Notably, dominance is found to be more salient to the concept represented by the term "anger," and humiliation and helplessness are found to be more salient to the concept represented by the term "hate." Perhaps, when an offense that would typically precipitate anger is compounded by a perceived humiliation and impotence, hate emerges.

Another way utilized by prototype researchers to identify the features of emotion-scripts is by surveying the language that surrounds emotion terms. In a groundbreaking study of anger-scripts, George Lakoff and Zoltán Kövecses derive a coherent portrait of the concept of anger from the metaphors and metonymies for it. Based on English expressions such as "He was filled with anger" and "Try to get your anger out of your system," they suggest that anger is conceived as a substance that fills the body but is eventually discharged from it. Based on expressions such as "You make my blood boil," "His pent-up anger welled up inside of him," "We got a rise out of him," "Smoke was coming out of his ears," "I could barely contain my rage," and "She blew up at me," they suggest

6 *Introduction*

that anger is conceived as a hot fluid that produces rising steam and eventually explodes.[21]

Interviews of native English-speakers, coupled with surveys of anger metaphors, converge to reveal the following anger-script: an offending event precipitates anger; the subject attempts to control anger; however, the subject loses control. Metaphorically this sequence of events is conceived as follows: a hot fluid fills body; the body is unable to contain the rising stream; the steam causes an explosion out of the body.

While other cultures possess terms whose meanings are similar to "anger," their scripts may be different. This is apparent, for example, when we compare English "anger" with Chinese *nu*. On the one hand, the metaphor of anger as contained in the body appears to be cross-cultural, likely the result of a common universal human experience of embodiment. Chinese *nu* is predicated on the notion *qi*, which, like English anger, is conceived as a substance that fills the body in response to an offense. Hence, we find Chinese expressions such as "to have one's cavities filled with anger" (*man qiang fen nu*).[22]

On the other hand, Chinese expressions suggest that *nu* is not, like anger, typically discharged in a loss of control. Rather, it is conceived as a fluid or gas that flows or moves through the body until it is released in an intentional and self-directed manner, or is diverted to and experienced somatically in various parts of the body (e.g., breast, heart, head, stomach, and spleen). Hence, we find Chinese expressions such as "to move one's anger" (*dong nu*) and "the anger in one's heart" (*xin zhong de nuqi shizhong wei neng Pingxi*).[23] The different expressions of anger and *nu* indicate that a loss of control and heat are more central to anger than they are to *nu*, and certain somatic experiences are more central to *nu* than they are to anger.

Variants

Some researchers view an emotion-script as the "primary," or even "privileged," conceptual representation of an emotion concept, and they view divergences from it—"variants"—as "abnormal" or "irregular" representations of it. This is not the case.[24]

An emotion-script describes an idealized model, or the "best example" of an emotion absent any context. Actual instances of an emotion—be they imagined or encountered—cannot be identical to an idealized model because they are contextualized and therefore possess additional details not represented in the prototype. James Russell and Beverly Fehr express this point using the example of anger:

> When no context is specified, the word anger recalls its own prototypical context: One person offends another. The offended

person is overwhelmed with feelings, impulses, and sensations. He (and we think the prototypical angry person is a man) glares, clenches, struggles to control his anger, and then lashes out in violence. But the script is such that somewhat different sequences are recalled when more context is specified. A young man "angry at the world" recalls a more brooding, irritable person, subject perhaps to bouts of self-destructive behavior. An angry infant may respond simply to frustration with loud crying. An angry politician may give impassioned speeches.[25]

According to this understanding, a variant is not an irregular instance of an emotion; on the contrary, all instances of an emotion are variants. This is because all instances of an emotion overlap with the idealized model while also possessing additional contextual details. Some of these details may be unique to the particular instance, while others may be elements of an emotion-script that covers a narrower set of cases. For example, the prototype of "a young man angry at the world" is a variant of the broader anger-script. It evokes a distinct sequence of prototypical traits that overlaps with the broader model of anger but covers a smaller set of contexts—a more brooding, irritable person, subject perhaps to bouts of self-destructive behavior.

Briefly put, the specific way an instance of an emotion diverges from the course anticipated by a prototypical script—be it a broader emotion-script or a narrower variant of that script—reveals the unique tenors of the emotion in that specific instance.

Biblical Emotion Terms

The prototype approach that is applied to the modern study of emotion concepts can be fruitfully applied to the study of biblical emotions. The method of inquiry must differ, however, because researchers cannot interview groups of ancient Hebrew-speakers in the same way they can interview modern English-speakers.

Fortunately, the Bible is a kind of informant in its own right. The corpus of biblical literature was composed by multiple authors who lived in different locations and at different times. As such, biblical representations of emotions, especially emotions attested across multiple books, likely reflect broader ancient Israelite emotion concepts. To be fair, one could argue that the Bible was composed by a narrow pool of literate members of ancient Israelite society, whose perspectives do not necessarily reflect majority viewpoints. Even so, these ancient composers shared a common language and larger sociocultural context with their nonliterate peers. Accordingly, their concepts of emotions are likely reflective of wider notions.

8 *Introduction*

   Considering biblical emotion terms against the background of modern English emotion terms is challenging for another reason as well. English-speakers readily identify terms such as happiness, anger, sadness, hate, and jealousy as members of the superordinate EMOTION category. The biblical Hebrew lexicon does not contain a term that is delimited in the same ways as the English term "emotion." In other words, there is no term for "emotion," such as we understand it in biblical Hebrew.

   Wierzbicka defines EMOTION as follows: "The English word emotion combines in its meaning a reference to 'feeling,' a reference to 'thinking,' and a reference to a person's body."[26] By contrast, the roots that biblical translators typically equate with modern emotion terms represent, as Françoise Mirguet explains it, amalgamations of "traits that English-speakers typically distinguish," including "actions, movements, ritual gestures and physical sensations."[27] In fact, since biblical Hebrew does not possess an equivalent category to English EMOTION, terms such as *ḥrh*, *śn'*, *yr'*, *'hb*, and *qn'* may not even be conceived as members of the same conceptual category.

Biblical *Śn'* and *Ḥrh*-Scripts and Their Variants

Among the terms that biblical translators typically equate with modern emotion terms, the roots *śn'* and *ḥrh* emerge as an especially suitable pair to study. Both terms are attested frequently and across diverse biblical books and genres. This provides a wide evidence base upon which to distinguish traits that are central to the concepts of *śn'* and *ḥrh*, more broadly, from those that are central to the concepts in a narrower literary context.[28]

   In addition, the lexemes often appear in the same passage and have similar connotations. Yet they each possess traits that are more central to one than to the other. For instance, *śn'*- and *ḥrh*-scripts both describe a response to an offense that is followed by an aggressive action; however, *ḥrh* typically targets offenders, and *śn'* typically targets the innocent.[29] This difference suggests that dominance is more central to the concept of *ḥrh* than it is to the concept of *śn'*.

   Finally, since English translators so often equate *śn'* with hate and *ḥrh* with anger, we can be relatively certain that a conceptual overlap exists between Hebrew and English. Overlap is not surprising, since the Bible seeks to portray the human experience, and, indeed, some elements of human emotions are universal. Nonetheless, other elements of emotions are culturally determined, and a vast cultural divide separates those who spoke ancient Hebrew from modern English-speakers. Consequently, we cannot presume that the English definitions of hate and anger can map perfectly onto *śn'* and *ḥrh*.

Since we cannot rely entirely on our understanding of the English language, we must unpack the meanings on *sn'* and *ḫrh* on their own terms. Classical theorists would argue that we can best understand the meanings of *sn'* and *ḫrh* by identifying their essential traits. Yet when we survey the Hebrew Bible in search of defining traits, we find only typical traits. *Sn'* tends to arise in response to a perceived wrongdoing and may incite injury, but it sometimes occurs absent perceived wrongdoing and does not provoke injury. *Ḥrh* is usually ascribed to parties with "power, status, and stature" who are responding to disregard for their authority; but periodically, it describes the response of a disempowered party. Therefore, rather than searching for necessary traits, which, prototype theorists argue, do not exist anyway, a more productive approach is to identify the emotion-scripts that elicit their attestations.

We refer to the widest range of traits that elicits attestations of *sn'* and *ḫrh* as the Broad Biblical *Sn'*- and *Ḥrh*-Scripts. The sequence of traits that is central to both of them, as evidenced by its frequency and pervasiveness across biblical collections, is of a socially dominant subject who targets another for aggressive action. The centrality of a social dynamic of dominance suggests that both *sn'* and *ḫrh* connote a privilege of social standing that distinguishes these terms from English hate and anger.

Importantly, the Broad Biblical *Sn'*- and *Ḥrh*-Scripts are idealized models, not definitions. They describe "best examples" of *sn'* and *ḫrh* absent any details about context. *Actual* examples of *sn'* and *ḫrh* overlap with these idealized models, while also possessing details related to their specific contexts. In some cases, these details converge to form variant *sn'* and *ḫrh*-scripts that apply to narrower sets of passages.

For example, across biblical narratives, we discern two variants of the Broad Biblical *Sn'*-Script (the Male-Targeted *Sn'*-Script and the Female-Targeted *Sn'*-Script) and two variants of the Broad Biblical *Ḥrh*-Script (the Outsider-Targeted *Ḥrh*-Script and the Kin-Targeted *Ḥrh*-Script). These variants incorporate details about the contexts of *sn'* and *ḫrh* that encourage a more nuanced view of the bearers of these emotions. Specifically, the *sn'*-scripts provide contextual details that focus on the moral standing of the hater, and the *ḫrh*-scripts offer details that direct attention to the legitimacy of the angered party's authority.

The Male-Targeted *Sn'*-Script introduces the hater as having been maltreated by another and depicts him appealing for help from his target; this encourages a more benevolent regard for the bearer of hate. By contrast, the Female-Targeted *Sn'*-Script portrays the target of *sn'* suffering interminably while her hater thrives—details that inspire a more disparaging view of the hater. We suggest that biblical narratives are more reproachful of *sn'* toward women due to the ease with which a man can use this privilege of power to take advantage of them.

10 *Introduction*

The Outsider-Targeted Ḥrh-Script portrays the angered party reasserting his authority over a compromised domain with a severe, and even lethal, act of aggression. By contrast, the Kin-Targeted *Ḥrh-Script* portrays *ḥrh* that is benign. Significantly, kin-targeted *ḥrh* foreshadows a greater loss of authority. A kin's disregard for authority is a sign that the family hierarchy is unstable, and the self-interest and affection that characterize kinship renders the angered party unprepared to act harshly enough to restore order and retain authority.

Across biblical poetry and prophetic literature, we discern three variants of the Broad Biblical *Sn'*-Script (i.e., the God-Targeted *Sn'*-Script, the Evil-Targeted *Sn'*-Script, and the Divine *Sn'*-Script) and three variants of the Broad Biblical Ḥrh-Script (i.e., the Divine Warrior *Hrh*-Script, the Synergistic Warrior *Ḥrh*-Script, and the Divine Kinsman *Ḥrh*-Script). In keeping with their broader models, these variant scripts direct attention to the themes of morality and authority, respectively.

As a group though, they diverge from the broader models of *sn'* and *ḥrh* to portray God as exceptional. The God-Targeted *Sn'*-Script portrays wicked haters succumbing to their targets, rather than dominating them; the Evil-Targeted *Sn'*-Script portrays *sn'* as a response to, and not the cause of, social injustice; and the Divine *Sn'*-Script uses conceptual transfer to focus attention on the sinfulness of God's target.

While Old Poetic and prophetic passages align with the Broad Biblical *Ḥrh*-Script in focusing on the theme of dominant authority, they reserve this role for God. The variant scripts characterize *ḥrh* as heat but, distinctively, describe this heat as a manifest fire with which God burns his targets. Finally, the Divine Kinsman Ḥrh-Script accords with its narrative counterpart (the Kin-Targeted *Ḥrh*-Script) in portraying *ḥrh* as tempered by kinship. However, God's temperance does not foreshadow a loss of authority; rather, it signifies Israel's imminent return to God.

While not all elements of the emotional experience are universal, some of them are. This is because human beings share, in common, an experience of the world through their physical bodies. Thus, we begin our study of *sn'* and *ḥrh* by unpacking the emotion-scripts of English terms that are most similar to them: hate and anger.

Notes

1 Jan Plamper, *History of Emotions: An Introduction* (Oxford: Oxford University Press, 2017), 151–72. William James, in his 1884 article "What Is an Emotion," argued that emotions are not the *cause* of physiological reactions,

Introduction 11

as Darwin seemed to suggest, but the *perception* of them; an event triggers a bodily change, which then produces a feeling—i.e., "emotion"; William James, "What Is an Emotion," *Mind* 9/34 (1884): 188–205. Cited in Plamper, *History of Emotions*, 175. As some point, one problem with viewing emotions as primarily physiological symptoms is the fact that symptoms may occur in contexts unrelated to mental states. For example, the same heart that races when afraid also races when running. What makes the former physiological experience an emotion and the latter not? See discussion in Plamper, *History of Emotions*, 179.

2 Ekman refers to these universal emotions as "basic emotions." While his list of basic emotions changed over time, it often included surprise, anger, fear, disgust, sadness, and joy; Paul Ekman, *Emotions Revealed: Recognizing Faces and Feelings to Improve Communication and Emotional Life*, 2d ed. (New York: Henry Holt, 2003), 1–16. Carol Izzard identifies joy, surprise, distress, anger, fear, shame, disgust, contempt, and guilt as universal emotions; Carol Izzard, *The Face of Emotion* (New York: Appleton-Century-Crofts, 1971).

3 While those who disagree with Ekman do not necessarily deny the existence of universal basic emotions altogether; they do argue that innateness is not the *only* explanation for emotions; see discussion in Plamper, *History of Emotions*, 151, 158–63.

4 Richard Lazarus, *Emotion and Adaptation* (New York: Oxford University Press, 1994). Lazarus was a leading figure in what became known as the Cognitive Theory, or the Appraisal School of Emotions, which gained traction as behaviorism was losing ground.

5 Lutz goes so far as to argue that emotions are not only influenced by culture, they are "*preeminently* cultural"; Catherine Lutz, *Unnatural Emotions: Everyday Sentiments on a Micronesian Atoll and Their Challenge to Western Theory* (Chicago: University of Chicago Press, 1988), 5–6. See also idem and Geoffrey White, "Anthropology of Emotions," *Annual Review of Anthropology* 15 (1986): 405–36.

6 Anna Wierzbicka, *Emotions across Languages and Cultures: Diversity and Universals* (Cambridge: Cambridge University Press, 1999), 123.

7 "Foreign Words without Literal English Translations: How to Use Them and Where They Might Come Up in the Workplace," blog.mangolanguages.com, Apr. 13, 2016.

8 Rom Harré, *The Social Construction of Emotions* (Oxford: Oxford University Press, 1986), 12. Cited in Paul Griffiths, *What Emotions Really Are: The Problem of Psychological Categories* (Chicago: University of Chicago Press, 1997), 159.

9 Anna Wierzbicka, "Human Emotions: Universal or Culture-Specific," *American Anthropologist* 88 (1986): 584.

10 Anna Wierzbicka, *Semantics, Culture, and Cognition: Universal Human Concepts in Culture-Specific Configurations* (New York: Oxford University Press, 1992), 125.

11 Wierzbicka, *Emotions across Languages and Cultures*, 306–7.

12 Wierzbicka, *Emotions across Languages and Cultures*, 306–7.

13 The classical approach to categorization can be traced back to Aristotle, who distinguished between essential traits that are the essence of an entity's nature and accidental traits that are incidental properties that play no part in determining that thing's nature; John Taylor, *Linguistic Categorization* (Oxford: Oxford University Press, 2003), 20–29.

12 Introduction

14 Taylor, *Linguistic Categorization*, 35–39.
15 See Eleanor Rosch's discussion, in "Cognitive Representations of Semantic Categories," *Journal of Experimental Psychology* 104 (1975): 192–235.
16 James Russell, "Culture and Categorization of Emotion," *Psychological Bulletin* 110 (1991): 442.
17 On emotion-scripts, see also John K. Rempel, Christopher T. Burris, and Darius Fathi, "Hate: Evidence for a Motivational Conceptualization," *Motivation and Emotion* 42 (2019): 179–90; Julie Fitness, "Anger in the Workplace: An Emotion Script Approach to Anger Episodes between Workers and Their Superiors, Coworkers, and Subordinates," *Journal of Organizational Behavior*, supp. special issue 21 (2000): 147–62; Julie Fitness and Garth J. O. Fletcher, "Love, Hate, Anger, and Jealousy in Close Relationships: A Prototype and Cognitive Appraisal Analysis," *Journal of Personality and Social Psychology* 65/5 (1993): 942–58; Russell, "Culture and Categorization," 426–50; Phillip Shaver et al., "Emotion Knowledge: Further Exploration of a Prototype Approach," *Journal of Personality and Social Psychology* 52/6 (1987): 1061–86.
18 Members of a common conceptual category may share a family resemblance because they are linked through a complex pattern of crisscrossing and overlapping attributes, but there are no clear boundaries separating members from nonmembers. The variety of ways a collection of traits may resemble an exemplar produces ambiguous cases, as James Russell and Beverly Fehr explain, using the example of anger: "Rather than properly defined, happiness, sadness, fear, anger, and other natural language categories of emotion are fuzzy: (a) Borders between categories are vague, rather than clear-cut. Although some actual events are clear cases of, for example, anger and other actual events are clearly not anger, some events straddle the fence and are difficult to decide one way or the other. (b) Membership within a category is a matter of degree rather than an all or none. Actual cases of anger vary in how well they exemplify the concept." James Russell and Beverly Fehr, "Fuzzy Concepts in a Fuzzy Hierarchy: Varieties of Anger," in *Journal of Personality and Social Psychology* 67/2 (1994): 186–205.
19 For example, Fitness and Fletcher, "Love, Hate, Anger, and Jealousy in Close Relationships"; Russell, "Culture and Categorization"; Shaver et al., "Emotion Knowledge."
20 Plamper, *History of Emotions*, 87, summarizing the findings of Ruth Benedict in her *The Chrysanthemum and the Sword*. Notably, *on* more frequently elicits suicide and intergenerational care than shame.
21 Metaphor can be understood as a way that human thought employs a more tangible domain of experience to understand a domain of experience that is less so. George Lakoff and Zoltán Kövecses, "The Cognitive Model of Anger Inherent in American English," in *Cultural Models in Language and Thought*, ed. Dorothy Holland and Naomi Quinn (Cambridge: Cambridge University Press, 1987), 195–221, esp. 198–203.
22 Zoltán Kövecses, *Metaphor and Emotion: Language, Culture, and Body in Human Feeling* (Cambridge: Cambridge University Press, 2003), 147.
23 Kövecses, *Metaphor and Emotion*, 151–52.
24 Russell and Fehr, "Fuzzy Concepts," 203.
25 Russell and Fehr, "Fuzzy Concepts," 202.
26 Wierzbicka, *Emotions across Languages and Cultures*, 3.
27 Françoise Mirguet, "What Is an 'Emotion' in the Hebrew Bible?" *Biblical Interpretation* 24 (2019): 443.

28 Ḥrh is not the only root used to describe an urge to harm that is precipitated by disregarded authority. However, it is, by far, the most common one. This is why we focus our study primarily on this term. Nonetheless, we do include synonyms of ḥrh (e.g., ḥmh and 'p) when they clearly represent an ḥrh-script and are a book's preferred root. On the nuances of various anger terms, see Grant, *Divine Anger in the Hebrew Bible*, 22–39.
29 G. Johannes Botterweck et al., "חרה ḥārâ," *Theological Dictionary of the Old Testament*, 5:171; E. Lipiński, "שנא śāné'," *Theological Dictionary of the Old Testament*, 14:164.

2 Discerning Modern Hate and Anger Scripts

Defining Hate and Anger

There is little consensus among psychologists and other researchers as to how to distinguish between hate and anger. In fact, there is little consensus as to how to define the emotions altogether.[1]

Hate has been categorized variously as an emotion, a syndrome, and even a disposition. It has been described paradoxically as an "adaptively antiquated anger" and as a "mental abnormality ... designed to rationalize the anxiety and torment of a demeaning existence."[2] Many agree that hate is not one emotion but a composite of several emotions. Yet there is little agreement on which emotions comprise hate. Some argue that hate is composed of anger and fear. Others say that it is composed of anger, disgust, and contempt. Still others view hate as a combination of fear, disgust, and contempt—but *not* anger.[3]

Some claim that anger is a physiological experience, while others argue that physiology is not even a component of it. Many agree that anger is a type of appraisal, but they do not agree on what kind; it has been variously viewed as a response to an appraisal of injustice, immorality, frustration, or danger. However, some point out that anger can occur for no reason at all.[4]

Efforts at offering comprehensive definitions of hate and anger have tended to be so elaborate as to belie their usefulness. In a notable example, Robert Sternberg argues that the concept of hate can be encompassed in three potential "action-feeling elements." The first is a negation of intimacy which arouses feelings of revulsion, disgust, and distancing. The second is passion which is expressed as either anger or fear and motivates either fighting or fleeing. The third is commitment which is expressed as contempt and a devaluing of the target.[5] The expansiveness of Sternberg's description begs the question: What negative experiences are not hate?[6]

In a similar vein, one expert defines anger as "an internal state involving varying degrees and interactions between physiological, affective, cognitive, motoric, and verbal components."[7] What, then, distinguishes anger from any other psychological state, let alone from another emotion?

Some researchers have sought to unpack the concepts of anger and hate by comparing emotions to one another, and it has long been recognized that the profiles of hate and anger are similar. Direct interviews and surveys find that both are often characterized by a desire to harm another and that they share similar physiological profiles. These include gastrointestinal discomfort, such as a tight stomach, a quickening pulse, high blood pressure, and feelings of being overcharged.[8]

And yet, while theorists recognize a conceptual overlap, there is little agreement over just how to interpret this overlap. Some experts suggest that the profiles are so similar because hate is a subtype of anger or a personalized form of anger. Aaron Beck, for instance, describes hate as an "outgrowth of anger that arises when a threat is perceived as persistently unjust, and a target as fixedly malicious."[9] Other experts argue just the opposite—hate is a more generalized version of anger.[10]

Fortunately, experts' theoretical definitions of hate and anger are not our primary interest. In the Bible, we confront a corpus of literature that was composed by numerous hands who resided in different locations and at different times. This suggests that the emotion concepts represented in the Bible were held by a large swath of ancient Israelite folk. Therefore, a better analogy to the biblical evidence than the opinions of experts (which do not necessarily mirror concepts held by a larger community) are the notions held by a cross-section of native English-speakers.[11]

In the twentieth century, researchers gained new insights into modern (Western-American) conceptions of hate and anger through interviews and surveys of native English-speakers.[12] By the end of the twentieth century, a subsection of these surveys was aimed at identifying the "best examples" which drive determinations about how speakers identify an instance of a particular emotion.

Prototypical Hate

Prototype studies of hate affirm some, but not all, of what earlier studies conclude about hate. Specifically, they identify three features as central to the conceptual model of hate: an impulse to harm, an urge to avoid, and a feeling of humiliation.[13]

Impulse to Harm

One of the earliest empirical investigations of conceptions of hate among laypersons was conducted in 1950 by Peter McKellar, who ran a series of interviews aimed at revealing the nature of "hostile attitudes":

> Each interviewee was asked to think about an incident involving him- or herself and the hated or otherwise disliked person. The

participant was then asked to imagine the "ideal resolution" of the incident and describe both his or her current feelings toward the "object of hostility" and how he or she would expect to feel and act toward this person upon encountering him or her in the vicinity of the interview room.[14]

Numerous subjects remarked that they wanted to harm the targets of their hate. One subject wanted her target to experience "exactly the same amount of pain, no more and no less, than the hater experienced." Another wished that her target would "cry the way she heard me." For McKellar, these statements (among others) testify to haters' central desire that their targets suffer retributively to the suffering they cause.[15]

In 1969, J. R. Davitz "sought to produce a 'dictionary of emotional meanings' [through] the validated consensus of contemporary laypersons." Toward this end, he instructed people to think of specific instances when they had experienced a given emotional state. Davitz's respondents associated hate with urges to harm, such as "to strike out ... kick, or bite."[16]

More recent prototype studies have affirmed some of the earlier conclusions of McKellar and Davitz, while adding more nuance. They found that an impulse to harm is, in fact, *more central* to the prototypical model of hate than are virtually all other traits, but, contrary to the earlier studies, retribution is not especially central to it.

In one series of studies, John Rempel, Christopher Burris, and Darius Fathi asked a set of subjects to define "what the word 'hate' means to them" and asked a different set of subjects to rate "how good an example of hate" is each of the definitions generated by the first group.[17] Participants were advised as follows:

> This study has to do with what we have in mind when we hear and use words. Consider the word "red." Close your eyes and imagine a true red. Now imagine an orangish red. Imagine a purplish red. Although you might still name the orange-red or the purple-red with the term "red," they are not as good examples of "red" (not as clear cases of what red refers to) as the clear, true red. Orange and purple are even poorer examples of "red," perhaps not even red at all. Notice that to judge how good an example something is has nothing to do with how much you like the thing. You might prefer a purple-red or purple to a true red, but still recognize which is the better example of "red." The word we are interested in is HATE. On the following page is a list of different kinds of hate. You will be asked how good an example of hate the various types or instances of hate are. Don't worry about why you think something is or isn't a good example. Just give us your opinion.[18]

Subjects rated "strong, clear motivational statements of desired or intended harm" as "most central" to hate. Specifically, the three statements that received the highest centrality ratings are "wishing death upon the target," "thought of murder," and "premeditated acts of violence and abuse." Among the top ten statements with the highest centrality rating are "a desire to destroy," "a strong emotion that creates the desire to harm," "a desire to make the target's life miserable," "a desire to kill," "wishing harm upon the target," and "acting maliciously towards the target."[19]

In a second study by these same researchers, subjects were asked to rate the degree to which twelve statements qualify as hate. Statements that describe an urge to harm received the highest centrality ratings. Examples include: "I want to hurt him. Period" and "I want him to be hurt, because society would be better off."[20]

Another set of prototype studies, which was aimed at distinguishing among several emotions in the context of marital relationships, affirmed that an urge to harm is central to people's conceptions of hate. Julie Fitness and Garth Fletcher asked married subjects to imagine a hypothetical scenario in which they might feel love, hate, anger, or jealousy toward their spouse:

> After being instructed to relax, subjects were asked to think of the most typical kind of event they believed would make one partner feel love, hate, jealousy, or anger toward the other in a marital relationship. Subjects were then asked to write a description of the eliciting event in as much detail as possible. A series of probing open-ended questions followed, inquiring about probable physiological symptoms, urges, cognitions, likelihood of emotional expression and how the emotion would most likely be expressed.[21]

The urge to "physically hurt the partner" received the highest percentage frequency of response among all the reported urges and was associated with hate more so than with other emotions.[22]

While digging into the causes of hate, several prototype studies find that, contrary to McKellar's earlier finding, retribution is not especially central to people's conceptions of hate. When Rempel, Burris, and Fathi presented respondents with scenarios that described abstract or retributive hate, they associated the former with hate more strongly than the latter. Specifically, subjects were asked to imagine what it would feel like to stand in the shoes of either the narrator or the target in these scenarios:

Nihilistic Hate: Very simply, I could see nothing good in them. There were times that I felt that everything would be better if they simply ceased to exist, but not before they suffered a lot. They seemed like a waste of space. There were

Redress: times when the worst harm I could possibly imagine still seemed too good for them. I sometimes felt that if every reminder that they ever existed were destroyed, the world would be a better place.
I wanted to show them that their behavior was just plain wrong, and that they shouldn't be allowed to do and say what they did and get away with it. I wanted to say and do things to them so that they would think twice before trying to hurt me or cross me ever again. There are basic ways that people are supposed to behave and I believe they went too far. I just felt that something had to be done to make things right. The world is a better place if they are held accountable and suffer consequences for what they did.[23]

The first scenario, which displays no clear reason for a subject wanting to harm a target, received a higher centrality rating than the second scenario, which frames the urge to harm as a form of just retaliation.[24] Though this study counters McKellar's finding that retribution is central to hate, both findings suggest that an urge to harm is central to the prototypical model of hate.

Urge to Avoid

Prototype studies suggest that the urge to avoid is also central to the conceptual model of hate, though perhaps less so than the impulse to harm. When Rempel, Burris, and Fathi asked subjects to rate the degree to which statements are good examples of hate, subjects rated statements of avoidance, such as "wishing for the target not to exist," "wanting to eliminate the target from your life," "repulsion," "wanting to exclude the target from your life," "aversion," and "disgust" as moderately central.[25]

Studies of intimate partners conducted by Fitness and Fletcher also found that avoidance is strongly linked to the concept of hate. When they instructed subjects to try to remember as many details as possible about "the most recent time they had felt either love, hate, anger, or jealousy (even if only mildly) for their partner," they strongly associated hate with the urge to avoid. In fact, they recalled feeling the "urge to leave the situation," "acting coldly," and "walking out" more often than they recalled any other behavior, including the urge to physically hurt their partners.[26]

While these results counter those that find that an urge to harm is *most* central to hate, they indicate, nonetheless, that an impulse to harm and an urge to avoid are both strongly linked to the concept represented by the term "hate."

Humiliation

Fitness and Fletcher found that humiliation is, by far, the most common elicitor of hate. When they asked subjects either to recall or imagine an instance of hate, respondents most frequently associated it with having been "badly treated, unsupported, or humiliated by their partner."[27]

Fitness produced similar results when she adapted this study to the workplace. She found that workers who described an episode of anger, coupled with humiliation, more frequently volunteered having also felt hate than workers who described anger but did not mention having been humiliated. The former group reported "feeling ashamed, humiliated, or embarrassed; feeling put down, diminished or ridiculed."[28]

Modern English Hate-Script

To date, prototype researchers have focused more on identifying the traits central to the conceptual ideal of hate than on discerning their sequence within a large hate-script. When taken collectively, though, the central traits, which are an impulse to harm, an urge to avoid, and a feeling of humiliation, suggest the following hate-script:

- Subject perceives offense
- Subject feels humiliated
- Hate
- Subject is motivated to harm and avoid the offender

Prototypical Anger

Prototype studies find that the traits most central to anger are organized sequentially in much the same way as a "playwright's script."[29] When testers asked respondents to recall an experience of interpersonal anger or a typical instance of anger, they described a cognitive antecedent, response, an attempt at self-control, and a loss of control.[30]

Cognitive Antecedent

Cognitive-appraisal theorists, such as Richard Lazarus, posit that an appraisal of blameworthiness is core to the definition of anger. As Lazarus sees it, anger arises when one party purposely thwarts a goal that is tied to another's ego identity. The angered party tends to attack the blameworthy agent, though to what extent he pursues the attack depends on his appraisal of a favorable outcome.[31]

The appraisal theory falls short, though, in seeing blameworthiness as core to anger. Individuals report being angry sometimes without knowing why they are angry or even for no reason at all. In fact, affect theorists argue that anger may be simultaneous to or even precede an appraisal of blame. The most we can say is that a blameworthy offense is central to the concept of anger, but not that it is defining of anger.

Several prototype studies affirm Lazarus's view, to an extent, in finding that the purposeful and illegitimate interference (usually by another) in the execution of plans or the attainment of a goal is a central, though not necessarily defining, trait of anger. One study found that the perception of having been treated unfairly or unjustly by another person is the most common elicitor of anger.[32] Reported common examples of antecedents include a reversal or sudden loss of power, status, or respect, or a violation of an expectation, frustration, or interruption of a goal-directed activity.[33]

Response

Researchers found that in a prototypical anger event, a cognitive antecedent is followed by an array of expressive, cognitive, and/or behavioral responses. In some studies, the most frequently reported responses include "verbally attacking the cause of anger" and "loud voice, yelling, screaming, shouting." Others frequently reported responses include "attacking something other than the cause of anger." Shaver et al. interpret these responses as aimed at rectifying "injustice, to reassert power or status, to frighten the offending person into compliance, and/or to restore the desired state of affairs." Respondents also frequently reported experiencing a "red, flushed face which suggests that physiological symptoms are indeed central, if not necessary."[34]

Control

Respondents in prototype studies typically reported an attempt to control their anger. These include "suppressing the anger; trying not to show or express it" and "redefining the situation or trying to view it in such a way that anger no longer is appropriate."[35] In a study of anger among romantic partners, Fitness and Fletcher found that respondents often reported trying to control their anger, usually because they saw it as "a destructive emotion."[36]

An Anger-Script's Conceptual Metaphor

Around the same time that prototype researchers were using interviews to discern anger-scripts, George Lakoff and Zoltán Kövecses were working to do the same through the study of metaphors and metonymies.

Discerning Modern Hate and Anger Scripts   21

They argue that although the variety of anger expressions may *seem* to convey different conceptual ideas about anger, metaphorical expressions of anger actually converge to reveal a common conceptual (and cultural) model.

Lakoff and Kövecses posit that anger is conceived, metaphorically, as a hot substance contained in the human body in the same way that a fluid fills a container. The substance rises to the head, until it settles in the nose and the mouth. The substance's heat exerts force on the body, but the subject exerts a counterforce to try to control it. Eventually, the intensity of anger rises above the limit of control and takes control of the subject who loses his/her judgment and pursues aggressive action. This is conceived metaphorically as heat building up within the container (the body) and eventually exploding.

The physiological effects of anger are increased body heat, increased internal pressure (blood pressure, muscular pressure), agitation, and interference with accurate perception. As anger increases, its physiological effects increase. There is a limit beyond which the physiological effects of anger impair normal functioning.[37]

The container model is reflected in expressions such as "he was filled with anger." The effects of hot anger rising within the body is reflected in expressions such as "don't get hot under the collar," "they were having a heated argument," and "you make my blood boil." The conception of anger as a force that puts pressure on the body that it tries to control is implied in expressions such as "she was shaking with anger," and "she suppressed her anger." Finally, the conception of anger as a hot explosion is reflected in expressions such as "he was bursting with anger," "she blew up at me," and "we won't tolerate any more of your outbursts."[38] At the last stage, the subject performs a retributive act against the target, rebalancing the scales. The intensity of anger drops to zero and anger ceases to exist.[39]

When we consider the conceptual metaphor for anger proposed by Lakoff and Kövecses against the background of prototype interview studies, the following anger-script emerges:

Script	Conceptual Metaphor
Stage 1: Offending event	
Stage 2: Anger	A hot substance fills the body
Stage 3: Attempt at control	The hot substance rises inside the body
Stage 4: Loss of control	The substance explodes out of the body
Stage 5: Act of retribution	

Importantly, this sequence does not describe the *necessary* course of anger; it reflects the *expected* course of anger that informs judgment of whether an instance—be it real or imagined—should be labeled an instance of anger. As Lakoff and Kövecses explain it, there is no core set of traits that all kinds of anger have in common. Instead, there is a "category of cognitive models with a prototypical model in the center."[40]

Actual instances of anger, referred to by many as "variants," overlap with the broadest idealized model but possess additional details that cover a smaller set of contexts. In this view, the anger-script delineated above, represents the broadest and least defined collection of traits that an English speaker would intuitively identify to categorize as anger. The ways that a specific example of anger diverges from the course anticipated by its prototypical script reveals its unique tenors in that particular instance.[41]

Hate Is Inhibited Anger

As we mentioned above, researchers have long recognized that the profiles of hate and anger overlap, but there is little consensus as to how to interpret the overlap.[42] Prototype studies suggest that in their idealized forms, both hate and anger are precipitated by offense and evoke an urge to harm.

Beyond this are some distinct differences. A social dynamic of dominance is more central to anger, whereas a dynamic of weakness is more central to hate. A series of studies performed by Fitness and Fletcher found that intimate partners who reported anger tended to recall feeling that they were more in control of the situation than were their significant others. By contrast, partners who reported hate tended to perceive the situation as unpredictable and have "little relative power in an interpersonal conflict." Subjects reporting anger also tended to blame the precipitating event on their significant other more so than on themselves. By contrast, subjects recalling hate tended to report themselves as more to blame and conceive themselves more negatively—as, for example, "weak" or "stupid."[43]

Humiliation and avoidance were also found to be more central to hate than they are to anger. When Fitness asked respondents to recall and describe a time when they felt "really angry with someone at work," subordinates—lower-power workers—were more likely to report hate toward superiors than the converse. Moreover, they tended to voluntarily report "moderate to high levels of hate for offenders, especially if the offences have involved humiliation, and their immediate reactions were to withdraw." They also tended to report an immediate reaction to withdraw. By contrast, angered superiors reported low levels of hate, did not appraise events as unfair, and reported "confronting behaviors in order to 'sort the situation out' or even in some cases, to intimidate subordinates and let them know 'who's' in charge." They also tended to feel that the anger event was adequately resolved.[44]

As Fitness interprets these differences, anger "has embedded in it the notion of a certain power" to confront one's transgressor, which is a power that superiors possess. By contrast, "lasting hostility" (hate) is more likely to develop from a perception of "powerlessness, and an inability to effectively retaliate against a transgressor," which subordinates possess.

These findings suggest that dominance is more central to the concept of anger than it is to the concept of hate. As one scholar sums up the findings of prototype studies, "when people are asked to report hate, they are essentially reporting a helpless, ineffectual, inhibited and 'too risky to stick my neck out' kind of anger."[45]

In short, when an offense that would typically precipitate anger is compounded by a perceived humiliation and impotence to act, a variant of anger develops; this is hate. As we will come to see, biblical *snʾ* and *ḥrh* reflect a similar, though not identical, relationship.

Notes

1 Since most biblical translators and scholars agree that the English term that is conceptually closest to שנא is "hate," a reasonable place to begin our study of שנא is with a study of its accepted English counterpart.
2 Edward Royzman, Clark McCauley, and Paul Rozin, "From Plato to Putnam: Four Ways to Think about Hate," in *The Psychology of Hate*, ed. Robert J. Sternberg (Washington, D.C.: APA, 2005), 5–8.
3 Royzman et al., "From Plato to Putnam," 6–7.
4 There have been many attempts to define the core features of anger. Some argue that anger is caused by a perception of blameworthiness. On the various opinions, see Russell and Fehr, "Fuzzy Concepts in a Fuzzy Hierarchy: Varieties of Anger," *Journal of Personality and Social Psychology* 67 (1994): 186–205; Paul Ekman, *Emotions Revealed* (New York: Henry Holt, 2003); Joseph de Rivera, *A Structural Theory of Emotion* (New York: International Universities Press, 1977); William Gaylin, *The Rage Within* (New York: Simon and Schuster, 1984); Averill, *Anger and Aggression: An Essay on Emotion* (New York: Springer, 1982).
5 Robert J. Sternberg, "Understanding and Combating Hate," in *The Psychology of Hate*, ed. idem, 37–49.
6 Over the years, various definitions of hate have been proposed. Some particularly influential works include Robert C. Solomon, *True to Our Feelings: What Our Emotions Are Really Telling Us* (New York: Oxford, 2008); Aaron Ben-Ze'ev, *The Subtlety of Emotions* (Cambridge: MIT Press, 2000), esp. 379–404; Aaron Beck, *Prisoners of Hate: The Cognitive Basis of Anger, Hostility, and Violence* (New York: HarperCollins,1999); Nico J. Frijda, *The Emotions* (New York: Cambridge, 1986). For a more recent theory and an evaluation of the state of study, see Berit Brogaard, *Hatred: Understanding Our Most Dangerous Emotion* (New York: Oxford, 2020).
7 B. S. Sharkin, "The Measurement and Treatment of Client Anger in Counseling," *Journal of Counseling and Development* 66/8 (1988): 361.

8   Royzman et al., "From Plato to Putnam," 7.
9   Beck, *Prisoners of Hate*, 44. Experts variously contend that hate is more irrational, more intense, and longer-enduring than anger. However, prototype studies find that hate and anger are associated with similar degrees of intensity and duration. J. Fitness and G. J. Fletcher, "Love, Hate, Anger, and Jealousy," *Journal of Personality and Social Psychology* 65 (1993): 944–50.
10 Rempel et al., "Hate: Evidence for a Motivational Conceptualization," *Motivation and Emotion* 43 (2019): 179.
11 Of course, experts' definitions of hate are expected to correspond, to a large degree, with laypersons' conceptions of the meaning of the term "hate." This is especially the case when experts attempt to define hate according to how laypersons generally conceive of it and because many researchers are also members of the English-speaking community.
12 Royzman et al., "From Plato to Putnam," 11–12. See J. R. Davitz, *The Language of Emotion* (New York: Academic Press, 1969); Peter McKellar, "Provocation to Anger and the Development of Attitudes of Hostility," *British Journal of Psychology* 40/3 (1950): 104–14.
13 Rempel et al., "Hate: Evidence for a Motivational Conceptualization"; J. Fitness, "Anger in the Workplace: An Emotion Script Approach to Anger Episodes between Workers and Their Superiors, Co-workers and subordinates," *Journal of Organizational Behavior* 21 (2000): 147–62; Fitness and Fletcher, "Love, Hate, Anger, and Jealousy in Close Relationships"; James A. Russell, "Culture and Categorization of Emotions," *Psychological Bulletin* 110 (1991): 426–50; Phillip Shaver et al., "Emotion Knowledge: Further Exploration of a Prototype Approach," *Journal of Personality and Social Psychology* 52/6 (1987): 1061–86.
14 McKellar, "Provocation to Anger."
15 McKellar, "Provocation to Anger," 110.
16 Davitz, *The Language of Emotion*, 50.
17 Rempel et al., "Hate: Evidence for a Motivational Conceptualization."
18 Rempel et al., "Hate: Evidence for a Motivational Conceptualization," 182.
19 The researchers adopted their interview questions from Russell and Fehr, "Fuzzy Concepts in a Fuzzy Hierarchy," 190–93. They derived 213 hate statements from the first group and chose the top fifty-two hate statements to test on the second group. The second group was asked to rate each of the fifty-two statements on a goodness-of-example scale of 1–6. Rempel et al., "Hate: Evidence for a Motivational Conceptualization," 182–83.
20 Rempel et al., "Hate: Evidence of a Motivational Conceptualization," 184–85.
21 Study 2 in Fitness and Fletcher, "Love, Hate, Anger, and Jealousy," 950.
22 An urge to physically injure the target was found to be more central than even "hurting the third party" and "leaving the situation." This stands in contrast to Fitness and Fletcher's findings on recalled hate, of which the most commonly cited urges and behaviors are to leave the situation and act coldly, as we will discuss below.
23 Rempel et al., "Hate: Evidence for a Motivational Conceptualization," 185–87.
24 Centrality ratings were even higher when subjects explicitly referenced harm while justifying their ratings.
25 The hate statements were generated by a different set of subjects. Rempel et al., "Hate: Evidence for a Motivational Conceptualization," 182–87.
26 After being asked this, subjects were then asked "a series of open-ended questions designed to cue their memories for various aspects of the emotional experience: when the incident had happened; previous mood and post-mood;

remembered cognitions, verbal expressions, physiological symptoms, urges, behaviors, and control strategies and partner reaction were included." Fitness and Fletcher, "Love, Hate, Anger, and Jealousy," 944.
27 Fitness and Fletcher, "Love, Hate, Anger and Jealousy," 944–50.
28 Fitness, "Anger in the Workplace."
29 Russell, "Culture and Categorization," 442.
30 Studies that take a prototype approach to anger include George Lakoff, *Women, Fire, and Dangerous Things: What Categories Reveal about the Mind* (Chicago: University of Chicago Press, 2008), 381–401; Agneta Fischer, Antony Manstead, and Patricia Rodriguez Mosquera, "The Role of Honour-Related vs. Individualistic Values in Conceptualizing Pride, Shame, and Anger: Spanish and Dutch Cultural Prototypes," *Cognition and Emotion* 13/2 (1999): 149–79; Fitness, "Anger in the Workplace"; Fehr and Baldwin, "Prototype and Script Analysis of Laypeople's Knowledge of Anger," in *Knowledge Structures in Close Relationships: A Social Psychological Approach*, ed. Gary Fletcher and Julie Fitness (New York: Psychology Press, 1996); Russell and Fehr, "Fuzzy Concepts in a Fuzzy Hierarchy," 186–205; Fitness and Fletcher, "Love, Hate, Anger, and Jealousy"; Shaver et al., "Emotion Knowledge"; Zoltán Kövecses, *Metaphors of Anger, Pride, and Love: A Lexical Approach to the Structure of Concepts* (Amsterdam: John Benjamins, 1986).
31 Lazarus posits that anger's "core relational theme" is "a demeaning offense against me and mine." A number of late twentieth-century cognitive-appraisal theorists viewed emotions as patterned processes of appraisal of one's environment and action tendencies. Craig Smith and Phoebe Ellsworth, "Patterns of Cognitive Appraisal in Emotion," *Journal of Personality and Social Psychology* 48/4 (1985): 813–38; Frijda, *The Emotions*. On anger, in particular, see Raymond Giuseppe and Jeffrey Froh, "What Cognitions Predict State Anger?" *Journal of Rational-Emotive and Cognitive-Behavior Therapy* 20 (2002): 133–35; Gerald Clore et al., "Where Does Anger Dwell?" in *Perspectives on Anger and Emotion*, ed. Wyer and Srull (New York: Psychology Press, 2014), 1–46; G. L. Clore and A. Ortony, "What More Is There to Emotional Concepts than Prototypes?" *Journal of Personality and Social Psychology* 60 (1991): 48–50.
32 Also common in order of frequency of reporting were violation of an expected social convention (e.g., being lied to, having rights violated, or negligence) facilitating an undesirable outcome (e.g., getting what was not wanted, not getting what was wanted) and a perception that the "situation is unfair, wrong, not the way it is supposed to be." M. F. Mascolo and J. C. Mancuso, "Prototype Representations of Anger, Sadness, and Joy Concepts," unpublished ms., cited in Fehr and Baldwin, "Prototype and Script Analysis of Laypeople's Knowledge of Anger," 226–27.
33 In Shaver et al.'s study, respondents singled out blameworthiness more frequently than other antecedents. In fact, judgment of illegitimacy occurred in 95 percent of self-anger accounts. This suggests that blameworthiness is more central to the concept of anger than are other traits, which were brought up less frequently. Shaver et al., "Emotion Knowledge," 1077–79.
34 Shaver et al., "Emotion Knowledge," 1075, 1078, 1081. Theorists who argue for universal basic emotions single out physiological symptoms such as tight muscles and increased heart rate as defining of anger.
35 Shaver et al., "Emotion Knowledge," 1078.
36 Similar findings were derived when respondents were asked to conjure a typical anger scenario. A major difference lay only with attempt at control, which was described more often in a typical case than in the self-case. Testers

26 *Discerning Modern Hate and Anger Scripts*

suggested that this is due to the social expectations. Fitness and Fletcher, "Love, Hate, Anger, and Jealousy," 947–48.

37 Lakoff and Kövecses, "The Cognitive Model of Anger Inherent in American English," in *Cultural Models in Language and Thought*, eds. Holland and Quinn (Cambridge: Cambridge University Press, 1987), 196. According to Lakoff and Kövecses, metaphors and metonymies of anger reflect the conception that the (perceived) physiological effects of anger stand for anger.

38 Lakoff and Kövecses, "The Cognitive Model of Anger Inherent in American English," 196.

39 Subsequent to his study of modern English anger, Kövecses widened his scope to compare and contrast English, Chinese, Japanese, and Hungarian anger-scripts. Kövecses found that all four languages share a common anger-script, which includes a physiological element and comprises several successive stages: anger is caused by a certain situation; the subject attempts to control it; the subject loses control; the subject expresses anger. The conceptual metaphor that underlies this script is that of "a force inside the person that can exert pressure on him or her" and ultimately interferes with "normal mental functioning." Kövecses posits that the "four cultures seem to conceptualize human beings as containers, and anger or its counterpart as some kind of substance (a fluid or gas) inside the container." As examples, Kövecses translates a number of expressions, including "full cavity anger" (Chinese), "anger in my body to be filled was" (Japanese), and "he is full of anger" (Hungarian). He points out, as well, that the languages all signal a conception of anger as a kind of hot substance; hence the expressions "one's intestines are boiled" (Japanese) and "boiled in him the anger" (Hungarian). Finally, the languages share a common view that the container can explode from the hot pressure, which he ascribes to the shared human experience of embodiment.

Kövecses asserts, nonetheless, that culturally specific concerns affect how the container model is conceived and elaborated upon in different languages. He points to the Japanese conception, which includes increasing degrees of anger that correspond to metaphors for controlling it. For example, in Japanese, anger that has risen to the chest can still be overcome or hidden by smiling. But once it has risen higher than this, it cannot. Kövecses suggests that these entailments reflect the Japanese concern with, and emphasis on hiding and controlling, one's anger. Kövecses, *Metaphor and Emotion*, 15.

40 These deviations from this script do not reflect novel conceptual models but rather variants of the prototypical scenario. Lakoff and Kövecses, "The Cognitive Model of Anger Inherent in American English," 218.

41 Such is the case of the hothead. It bears a family resemblance to the anger-script, for it conjures a heat that fills the human body; but it does not overlap with the exemplar entirely, for it also presumes a body that is usually, or more quickly, filled with heat. In short, it is a variant of the broader model.

42 Rempel et al., "Hate: A Motivational Conceptualization," 179.

43 Anger and hate share some prototypical features, such as muscle tension. Intriguingly, however, Fitness and Fletcher found the hate-anger relationship to be asymmetrical. Subjects tended to confuse hate with anger when hate was the target emotion, but they did not experience the same difficulty in discriminating anger from hate when anger was the target emotion. Specifically, information identified (by an earlier study) as prototypical of hate led a number of subjects to incorrectly identify the target emotion as anger, but subjects did not confuse collections of features identified as prototypical anger with hate. One explanation for this is that the prototypical hate features obtained from

recall accounts in Study 1 represent elements of a more inclusive anger-script or prototype. This is in accord with Shaver et al.'s assertion that emotion concepts are arranged hierarchically, with anger being a more basic emotion concept than hate. Consequently, prototypical features relevant to hate may be subsumed within the broader anger category. Fitness and Fletcher, "Love, Hate, Anger, and Jealousy," 951–57.

44 Fehr and Baldwin suggest that anger-scripts may vary across gender, though they found that men and women both conceive anger as triggered by a betrayal-of-trust event; Fehr and Baldwin, "Prototype and Script Analysis of Laypeople's Knowledge of Anger," 230–40.

45 Fitness and Fletcher, "Love, Hate, Anger, and Jealousy," 955. They also found considerable overlap in responses for hate and anger in marital relationships (953). Fitness found no difference in the intensity or duration of anger and hate, which suggests that neither element is a key distinguishing feature of anger. Fitness, "Anger in the Workplace," 93. The theory that hate is an inhibited form of anger is further affirmed in a study by Fitness and Fletcher wherein respondents frequently mistook cases of hate as anger but only rarely mistook cases of anger as hate. From this, Fitness and Fletcher infer that hate falls within "elements of a more inclusive anger script or prototype."

3 Broad Biblical *Sn'*-Script

History of the Study of Biblical *Sn'*

Most English translations of the Hebrew Bible translate *sn'* as "hate." This is not surprising, since, in a lot of ways, biblical *sn'* resembles English "hate." Sometimes, though, translations equate *sn'* with various other English terms. For example, the ethical precept in Proverbs 11 (רַע־יֵרוֹעַ כִּי־עָרַב זָר וְשֹׂנֵא תֹקְעִים בּוֹטֵחַ, 11:5) has been diversely translated as follows:

> He who gives surety for a stranger will smart for it, but he who **hates** suretyship is secure.
>
> (RSV)

> To guarantee loans for a stranger brings trouble, but there is safety in **refusing** to do so.
>
> (NRS)

> Harm awaits him who stands surety for another; he who **spurns** pledging shall be secure.
>
> (TNK)

So, too, Jacob's *sn'* toward Leah in Genesis (כִּי־שְׂנוּאָה לֵאָה וַיִּפְתַּח אֶת־רַחְמָהּ וְרָחֵל עֲקָרָה וַיַּרְא יְהוָה, Gen 29:30) is variously translated thus:

> When Yahweh saw that Leah was **unloved**, he opened her womb, while Rachel remained barren.
>
> (NJB)

> When the Lord saw that Leah was **not loved**, he enabled her to conceive, but Rachel remained childless.
>
> (NIV)

DOI: 10.4324/9781003348719-3

When the LORD saw that Leah was **hated**, he opened her womb; but Rachel was barren.

(RSV)

Later, the Lord noticed that Leah was **being neglected**, so he made her fertile, while Rachel remained childless.

(ISV)

But the Lord, seeing that he **despised** Leah, opened her womb, but her sister remained barren.

(Catholic Public Domain Version)

A lack of agreement over how to define the root is evident also in the expansive definitions of *sn'* offered by modern lexica. According to one influential dictionary, the semantic scope of *sn'* spans from strongly affective "hate" to somewhat diluted "feel aversion for, not want, avoid":

> The gamut of feelings of dislike are to be included in the scope of שנא; it may express the most intense hatred of enemies of God (Ps 139:21–22), or that of a violent enemy (25:9), but it may simply express that which is to be avoided, such as serving as a guarantor for a debt (Prov 11:15), the feelings of aversion for a poor man (19:7). ... But on a less intense scale, hate may simply express the feelings of affection for one wife in contrast to the aversion for another.
>
> (Deut 21:15, 17)[1]

The few in-depth studies of *sn'* offer similarly broad definitions. Gene Brice, the first modern biblical scholar to offer a detailed study of *sn'*, posits that the lexeme "ranges in meaning from an objective expression of a covenantal abrogation and a technical meaning of divorce ... to the more emotional meanings, ranging from intense personal antipathy to complete indifference."[2] Robert Branson cautions, likewise, that the meaning of *sn'* in a given passage hinges on the degree to which the term connotes an emotion, a non-emotive action or state, or a meld of the two.[3]

In a recent lexical study, Andrew Riley locates individual examples of *sn'* on a "meaning continuum" that ranges from "literal" to "metaphorical." As Riley sees it, *sn'* tends to denote a "literal negative sentiment" when associated with jealousy or physical aggression, but it inclines toward the metaphorical when associated with divorce or abrogated covenant.[4] It is indeed important to recognize, as Riley does, that some passages foreground the emotive sense of *sn'* while others underscore its non-emotive connotations. In fact, *sn'* may carry multiple cognitive associations simultaneously, including both affective and non-emotive traits. The task of the biblical interpreter is to identify, for a given passage, which traits of *sn'* are emphasized over others, and why they are so.[5]

Prototype Approach to Biblical *Sn'*

The prototype approach, which researchers take toward identifying the prototypical traits of English hate, offers a way to understand *sn'*. As we have seen, prototype researchers use informant interviews to identify the traits most central to hate. These include an impulse to harm, an urge to avoid, and humiliation.

Biblical interpreters cannot interview groups of ancient Hebrew-speakers. But we can survey the traits typically associated with these terms. Classical theorists, who posit that people recognize and categorize concepts by their necessary traits, would have us understand the concept of *sn'* by identifying its essential traits. Yet as we have mentioned, when we survey attestations of *sn'* across the Hebrew Bible in search of any defining traits, we find only *typical* traits.

The prototype approach to emotion concepts explains this trend. In this view, the idealized model of *sn'* (its prototype) is characterized by traits strongly associated with, but not necessary to, its definition. As such, attestations of *sn'* may bear family resemblances to one another because they tend to share overlapping traits, but they are not identical because they do not necessarily share the same sets of overlapping traits.

Broad Biblical *Sn'*-Script

The traits most central to the "best example" of *sn'*, as indicated by their frequency and their pervasiveness across the Hebrew Bible, are dominance over the target, an urge to harm, an impulse to avoid, and a negative regard.[6] We refer to the sequence of traits that forms the conceptual model of *sn'* as the Broad Biblical *Sn'*-Script. It is as follows:

- Subject hates the less powerful and innocent target
- Subject harms the target
- Subject estranges the target
- Subject achieves no gains

In short, the prototypical *sn'*-script describes a dominant hater who hates a vulnerable target—one who is innocent of wrongdoing.[7]

As we saw in Chapter 2, the urge to harm and impulse to avoid are central to modern hate as well. However, hate anticipates a less powerful subject and a more powerful target, and *sn'* anticipates just the opposite: a more powerful party and a vulnerable target. This is expressed in groups hating individuals, kings hating subjects, and men hating women. The reverse does not apply. Individuals do not hate groups, subjects do not hate kings, and women do not hate men.

In an additional distinction, *sn'* anticipates a narrower scope of targets; *sn'* is typically directed at parties innocent of wrongdoing.

Importantly, the Broad Biblical *Sn'*-Script neither defines actual examples of hate, nor is it the only *sn'*-script in the Bible. It represents the idealized sequence of traits that is anticipated when no context is provided. Actual examples of *sn'* bear family resemblances to this broader conceptual model, but, as they are contextualized, they also possess details that might be central only to a narrower set of contexts, such as when hate targets a particular gender or is borne by God. In fact, actual instances of *sn'* possess details that are not central to a *sn'* script at all but are, rather, tethered to a specific example of *sn'*.

By recognizing the Broad Biblical *Sn'*-Script, we can appreciate the ways in which specific passages add to and diverge from it in distinctive ways.[8]

Notes

1 A. Konkel, "שנא," *NIDOTT*, 3:1257.
2 Gene Brice, "A Study of Hate and Anger in Old Testament Man" (PhD diss., Yale University, 1962), 5.
3 For example, Robert Branson initially argued that the lexeme is metaphorical for a broken covenant and not an indicator of negative emotion. He later moderated his view, suggesting that the breakdown of a covenantal relationship is the primary, not exclusive, meaning of *sn'* in most passages. "The Polyvalent *sn'*: An Emotional, Performative, and Covenantal Term," *Biblical Research* 51 (2007): 5–15. For more viewpoints, see Bruce Wells, "The Hated Wife in Deuteronomic Law," *Vetus Testamentum* 60/1 (2010): 131–46; Zvi Henri Szubin and Bezalel Porten, "The Status of a Repudiated Spouse: A New Interpretation of Kraeling," *Israel Law Review* 35/1 (2001): 46–78; Hélène Nutkowitz, "Concerning the Use of the Verb *Śn'* in Judaeo-Aramaic Contracts from Elephantine," *Journal of Semitic Studies* 52/2 (2007): 211–25.
4 Andrew J. Riley, *Divine and Human Hate in the Ancient Near East: A Lexical Contextual Analysis* (Piscataway: Gorgias, 2017).
5 Andreas Wagner takes a multidisciplinary approach to hate, considering hate against the background of German *Emotionen, Gefühle und Sprache im Alten Testament: Vier Studien* (Waltrop: Hartmut Spenner, 2006).
6 For lists of citations, refer to subsequent chapters.
7 In contrast to love, which motivates subjects to help others, hate motivates subjects to harm and actively avoid their targets.

32   Broad Biblical Sn'-Script

8 Traits can be central to a narrow *sn'*-script but not to the broadest one. For example, biblical poetry frequently associates *sn'* with battle imagery, equating the nominal form of *sn'* with "enemies." However, the association of haters with enemies is infrequent in biblical narratives. Haters are enemies—Exod 1:10; Lev 26:17; Esther 9; Exod 23:5; 2 Sam 22:18; Psalms 18; Ps 18:41; Ps 25:19; Ps 35:19; Ps 38:19; Ps 44:8, 10; Ps 55:13; Ps 69:5; Ps 83:3; Ps 89:24; Ps 105:25; Ps 106:10; Ps 139:22; Ezekiel 16, 27, 37; 23:28; Enemies of God—Num 10:35; Deut 32:41; Deut 33:11; Ps 21:9; Ps 68:10.

This does not mean that the connotation is altogether absent from the concept of *sn'* in biblical narratives. It simply means that the association is *less* central to the concept of *sn'* in narrative contexts than it is to an idealized model of *sn'* in poetic settings. Moreover, since the equation of haters and enemies is widespread only in poetry, the association is not especially central to the broader biblical *sn'*-script.

4 Narrative *Sn'*-Scripts

Male-Targeted *Sn'*-Script

- Subject is maltreated by the more dominant party.
- Subject hates the less powerful and innocent party.
- Subject seeks to avoid the target.
- Subject seeks to hurt the target.
- Subject seeks reconciliation and aid from the target.

Female-Targeted *Sn'*-Script

- Subject is maltreated by a more dominant party.
- Subject hates the less powerful and innocent target.
- Subject seeks to avoids the target.
- Subject seeks to harm the target.
- Target suffers and hater thrives.

We find two prominent variants of the Broad Biblical *Sn'*-Script in biblical narratives: the Male-Targeted *Sn'*-Script and the Female-Targeted *Sn'*-Script. They overlap with the more expansive script in some ways and diverge from it in others. All three scripts feature a dominant hater, an impulse to harm, and an urge to avoid. But the narrative scripts attest a trait that is not common to *sn'* outside of biblical narratives: an antecedent.

In biblical narratives, *sn'* is aroused when one party is maltreated or diminished by another against whom one cannot retaliate. The offended party directs *sn'* not at their more powerful perpetrator but at a vulnerable and innocent third party who (from the hater's perspective) benefits from their diminishment. By incorporating an antecedent, biblical narratives encourage a more benevolent assessment of the hater; the hater is regarded not just as an unjust perpetrator but also as a sympathetic victim.

The distinctive conclusion of the Male-Targeted *Sn'*-Script fosters even more sympathy for the hater; the hater is disempowered, repudiates

DOI: 10.4324/9781003348719-4

sn', and is compelled to appeal for help from his target. Surprisingly, the target is readily disposed to reconcile, even in case of absent recompense. The association of a loss of dominance with repudiated *sn'* along with the target's inclination to help his hater suggests that the concept represented by the term *sn'* is broader than the concept represented by the term "hate." *Sn'* connotes a gesture of a dominant social standing. The privilege of this gesture is rescinded when dominance is lost.

The Female-Targeted *Sn'*-Script does not follow the same trajectory. In stark contrast to male-targeted *sn'*, which ultimately resolves, female-targeted *sn'* typically results in interminable suffering. In fact, biblical narratives often juxtapose a woman's suffering against the contentedness of her male hater, casting *sn'* in an especially impugnable light. The Bible frequently exhorts against hurting those who hold a vulnerable social status, and women are typically of inferior standing. It is not surprising then that the Bible disparages taking advantage of one's social standing to target a woman with *sn'*.

To be clear, these variant *sn'*-scripts of biblical narratives are not actual examples of *sn'*; they are idealized models of *sn'* for a narrower scope of settings.[1] By identifying them, we can better discern toward what ends specific passages portray *sn'* in distinct ways.

Male-Targeted *Sn'*-Script

Joseph's Brothers (Genesis 37, 45)

Genesis 37 is an example of the Male-Targeted *Sn'*-Script. It distinguishes itself by especially foregrounding the antecedent of *sn'*. The sequence of events is as follows:

1 Jacob gifts a special garment to Joseph.
2 Joseph's brothers appraise Joseph as favored, at their expense.
3 Joseph's brothers hate Joseph.
4 Joseph's brothers estrange Joseph (abandon or sell him to servitude).
5 Joseph's brothers seek Joseph's reconciliation and help.

In keeping with the idealized model of *sn'* represented by the Broad Biblical *Sn'*-Script, a dominant party—Joseph's elder brothers—hates a vulnerable party: Joseph (וישנאו אתו, Gen 37:4). Joseph's vulnerability, as the youngest brother with the least clout, is underscored by the description of him as a mere *lad* (נער) relegated to attending the maidservants' sons (Gen 37:2).[2]

Prototypical of narrative *sn'*-, Genesis 37 offers an antecedent of *sn'*. The brothers hate Joseph because their father, Jacob, bestows upon him a distinctive garment, which demonstrates Jacob's preference for this younger son (37:3–5):

וישראל אהב את-יוסף מכל-בניו כי-בן-זקנים הוא לו עשה לו כתנת פסים: ויראו אחיו
כי-אתו אהב אביהם מכל-אחיו וישנאו אתו ולא יכלו דברו לשלם: ויחלם יוסף חלום ויגד
לאחיו ויוספו עוד שנא אתו:

The passage elaborates on this point. Joseph, who is a mere "lad," should serve his elder brothers. Yet Jacob elevates Joseph above his brothers by means of a conspicuous inheritance.[3] Joseph's "richly ornamented robe" is both an affront and a loss, for it signifies an elevation in Joseph's standing at the brothers' expense. This diminishment may not justify the brothers' acts of *sn'*; but at the very least, it arouses a modicum of sympathy for them.

As anticipated by the Male-Targeted *Sn'*-Script, the brothers do not direct their *sn'* at Jacob, the patriarch who diminishes them; instead, they hate Joseph, a vulnerable third party who benefits from their diminishment.

Also anticipated by the Male-Targeted *Sn'*-Script, the brothers' *sn'* precipitates a psychological and physical eschewal—they are unable to speak peaceably to Joseph (וישנאו אתו ולא יכלו דברו לשלם, 37:4). Claus Westermann interprets the absence שלם ("peace"), which is a greeting of welcome and farewell that also involves an inquiry into one's health and well-being, as a "rupture in the fellowship" between the brothers and Joseph.[4] The relational rift is realized in the next scene through a physical estrangement; the brothers shepherd together in the field without Joseph. This physical distancing of Joseph (37:12) may be intended to relieve the brothers' jealousy, which is mentioned immediately prior (37:11). Regardless, estranging Joseph does not restore the brothers' loss nor does it improve their lot; while the brothers are out in the fields, Joseph remains at home alone with their father, a setting that underscores Jacob's enduring favoritism of Joseph (37:12).

Thereafter, Jacob sends Joseph to seek out his brothers' well-being (ראה את-שלום אחיך, 37:14)—a directive that ironically augurs the violence to come. The passage has already made clear that Joseph's haters estranged him and they no longer wish him well (וישנאו אתו ולא יכלו דברו לשלם, 37:4). On the contrary, they are fixated on the threat that he poses and that his dreams foretell. The brothers' estrangement of, and narrow regard for, Joseph is on view when they confront him in the field and address him not as their brother but as "the dreamer" (הנה בעל החלמות הלזה בא, 37:19). In fact, the brothers refuse to acknowledge Joseph as kin, referring to him as Jacob's son (בנך) and not "our brother" (37:2), even when they falsely relay his death to their father.

Joseph's brothers subsequently exile him. With this act of hate, the brothers intend less to harm Joseph than to reclaim their loss or relieve the jealousy that accompanies it. This is evident in the two versions of the brothers' deliberations which are preserved in Genesis 37. In the first variant, Reuben suggests that they throw Joseph into a pit rather than kill him with their own hands, which would make them liable for his death (37:22). The other brothers assent. They mock ("and we shall see what will become of his dreams"; 37:20) and strip Joseph of the garment that Jacob gave him. Briefly put, the brothers are unwilling to risk liability for Joseph's murder (לא נכנו נפש, 37:21) but are willing to strip him of the garment that represents their own diminishment and exile him (37:23).

In the second variant, the brothers are quick to listen to Judah when he argues, similarly, that they sell Joseph to Ishmaelites rather than bear the guilt of fratricide (37:26–27). As in the first variant, the brothers are less interested in what becomes of Joseph than in profiting from his departure. Kenneth Mathews summarizes: "Murder and its cover-up will not pay as handsomely as a slave's price."[5] More accurately, they are interested in casting him out of the family in the most profitable way.

Even after describing this act of *sn'*, the narrator takes pains to cast the brothers somewhat sympathetically. Estranging Joseph does not garner Jacob's preferential treatment at all. On the contrary, the narrator asserts that Jacob lives out many days mourning for Joseph (37:34–35), presumably, instead of cherishing his sons thereafter.

The ensuing chapters describe a reversal of power that, ironically, was precipitated by the brothers. When famine strikes, Joseph rises to power in his place of exile, Egypt, and his brothers must entreat him for food and favor (Genesis 42–45). No longer empowered over Joseph, the brothers repudiate their *sn'* by performing the very same act that their *sn'* had earlier proscribed (37:4)—the brothers "speak" to him (כן דברו אחיו אתו, 45:15). They even address him as "like Pharaoh" (כי כמוך כפרעה, 44:18), acknowledging Joseph's dominance over them.[6]

Notably, Joseph does not punish the brothers for their *sn'*. Instead, after he is assured of their present piety (by refusing to abandon Benjamin), Joseph swiftly reconciles with them. He even offers to take care of their families in perpetuity (45:9–11). Joseph's eagerness to reconcile with his brothers suggests that while the brothers lost their privileged social standing to express *sn'*, he does not perceive their having acted on it as demanding recompense.

Jephthah's Brothers/Gileadites (Judg 11:1–11); the Philistines (Gen 26:13–32)

The attestations of *sn'* in Judges 11 and Genesis 26 include many traits prototypical of the narrative *sn'*-script while distinctively portraying the haters as unregretful. The sequence of traits proceeds as follows:

1 The father bears a son with a prostitute/outsider.
2 Jephthah's brothers fear that Jephthah diminishes their wealth.
3 Jephthah's brothers hate Jephthah.
4 Jephthah's brothers expel Jephthah to live among the rough/idle.
5 Jephthah's brothers/elders of Gilead seek Jephthah's military help.[7]
6 Jephthah agrees to be their military commander.

---

1 God blesses Isaac with riches.
2 Philistines envy Isaac.
3 Philistines stop up Isaac's wells.
4 Philistines hate Isaac.
5 Philistines (via King Abimelech) exile Isaac.
6 Philistines (via King Abimelech) seek a covenant of peace with Isaac.
7 Isaac prepares a feast and they cast a covenant.

Judges 11 and Genesis 26 share a number of traits in common with Genesis 37. All three narratives feature powerful parties who hate vulnerable ones. In Genesis 26, Isaac is living as a sojourner in a Philistine land during a time of famine and, consequently, is dependent on King Abimelech's goodwill (26:1). In Judges 11, Jephthah is the son of an outsider/prostitute, which, despite his being the eldest brother and a valiant warrior (11:1), is apparently a vulnerable enough status for the city elders to allow his brothers to exile him (11:2–3).[8]

Both Isaac and Jephthah describe themselves as exiled on account of *sn'* (אתם שנאתם אותי ותגרשוני מבית אבי, Gen 26:27; ואתם שנאתם אותי ותגרשוני מבית אבי, Judg 11:7). As anticipated by the narrative variants, in both passages, *sn'* is aroused by perceived diminishment or the threat thereof. Jephthah's brothers do not want "the son of another woman" to "inherit in our father's house" (11:2). Similarly, the Philistines are jealous of Isaac's relentless success and fear that his power threatens their well-being (26:14–16).[9]

In both passages, the targets of *sn'* are innocent of wrongdoing. It could be argued, even, that Jephthah has a claim to his father's inheritance and Isaac a claim to the land where he works. Any threat that Isaac poses stems from being a beneficiary of his deity's gifts (26:12–13). And were anyone a perpetrator, in Judges 11, it is Jephthah's father, who bore a child with a foreign woman and neglected to adjudicate among his sons.

As is distinct from the trajectory anticipated by the Broad Biblical *Sn'*-Script, *sn'* toward men concludes with a reversal of power and an appeal, by the hater, for reconciliation. Prior to granting this reconciliation, however, both Isaac and Jephthah question their haters. Responding to Abimelech's request to forge a covenant, Isaac asks (26:27–29):

ויאמר אלהם יצחק מדוע באתם אלי ואתם שנאתם אותי ותגרשוני מבית אבי ומדוע באתם
אלי עתה כאשר צר לכם: ויאמרו ראו ראינו כי-היה יהוה עמך ונאמר תהי נא אלה בינתינו
ביננו וביניך ונכרתה ברית עמך: אם-תעשה עמנו רעה כאשר לא נגענך וכאשר עשינו עמך
רק טוב ונשלחך בשלום אתה ברוך יהוה:

Jephthah poses a similar question to the elders of Gilead (11:6–7):

ויאמרו ליפתח לכה והייתה לנו לקצין ונלחמה בבני עמון: ויאמר יפתח לזקני גלעד הלא אתם שנאתם
אותי ותגרשוני מבית אבי ומדוע באתם אלי עתה כאשר צר לכם:

On the one hand, neither Jephthah's brothers nor Abimelech denies their *sn'*. On the other hand, they both claim to have meant their targets no harm. Abimelech argues not only that his people intended no harm but, quite the opposite, that they sent Isaac away in peace (בשלום, 26:29). The reference to peace in this *sn'* passage cleverly calls to mind Genesis 37, in which Joseph's brothers could not speak to him "in peace" when they hated him (בשלם; Gen 37:29). In fact, the entire argument resonates against the background of Genesis 37. Joseph did not begrudge the haters who exiled him; neither, then, should Isaac, who flourished in exile, hold a grudge against the Philistines (37:4, 25–28).

The elders of Gilead, in Judges 11, similarly refuse to acknowledge any wrongdoing. Instead, they simply repudiate their previous relationship and request that Jephthah become their head in battle against the Ammonites (11:8).

Both Isaac and Jephthah reconcile with their haters, despite receiving no admission of wrongdoing or recompense. Isaac forges a covenant with the Philistines, and, after some negotiation, Jephthah returns home to aid his countrymen. It appears that the dominant parties wield *sn'* with impunity, for even when they lose the privilege of their dominance, recompense does not follow.

Female-Targeted *Sn'*-Script

The Female-Targeted *Sn'*-Script overlaps widely with the Male-Targeted *Sn'*-Script. A point of departure, however, lies in its outcome. As we have seen, *sn'* toward men typically resolves. By contrast, *sn'* toward women typically concludes in suffering. Specifically, the hated woman suffers, while her male hater thrives. This outcome, especially as it differs from the outcome of *sn'* toward men, casts *sn'* toward women as particularly cruel. Typically lacking social capital, women were vulnerable and the Bible frequently exhorts against targeting the vulnerable. Portraying female-targeted *sn'* as especially reproachful is another, less explicit, way to exhort against taking advantage of the vulnerable.

Jacob (Gen 29:23–35); Samson (Judg 14:12–15)

Genesis 29 and Judges 14 describe haters avoiding their wives out of *sn'*. The former emphasizes the emotional desperation that can come of *sn'*, whereas the latter emphasizes the irrevocability of its consequence:

1 Laban tricks Jacob into marrying Leah.
2 Jacob hates Leah.
3 Leah suffers from Jacob's refusal to bond with her.

───────────────

1 Philistines coerce Samson's wife to trick him.
2 Samson slaughters the Philistines and leaves his wife in hate.
3 Samson burns the Philistines' foxes and land.
4 The Philistines burn Samson's wife and her father.

In accord with narrative *sn'*-scripts, Jacob hates Leah (כי-שנואה לאה, Gen 29:31, 33) even though the passage does not suggest that Leah offends Jacob in any way. Instead, the narrative relays how Laban deceives Jacob into marrying Leah in place of Rachel (29:13–28). The contiguity of Laban's deceit to Jacob's *sn'* implies that Jacob hates Leah because of Laban's action. Indeed, Jacob's distress seems justified, as Laban swindles seven years of Jacob's working life. Yet Jacob does not hate Laban, his superior and father-in-law; instead, he hates his innocent wife (כי-שנואה לאה, Gen 29:31, 33).

The emphasis of the rest of the passage lies in Leah's suffering. Some scholars argue that Jacob's *sn'* connotes a demotion of status rather than an intense emotion of hostility. They point out that Leah bears children with Jacob, arguing that a relationship characterized by "multiple sexual encounters" is not a hostile one. Instead, *sn'* is a metaphor for "demotion":

> In the Bible שנא appears frequently as a technical term with the meaning "to repudiate" or "demote." ... When juxtaposed to *hb*, "love" (= promotion to status of primacy), it often conveys the meaning of demotion, reduction of status ... the "hated" wife vis-à-vis "beloved." Though demoted, her children's

inheritance rights were preserved (Deut 21:15–17) .... The demoted wife remained within the matrimonial bond, akin to Leah, who became "hated." Having initially been Jacob's only wife, enjoying the status of primacy, she was demoted in status (Gen 29:31–33) upon the subsequent entrance into the household of Rachel as the beloved=preferred (i.e., first-ranking) wife.

(Gen 29:18, 20)[10]

While a demotion of status may be connoted by *sn'* (as is clearer in legal texts), it is not the primary thrust of this passage. Genesis 29 focuses, rather, on the distress that Jacob's refusal to bond with Leah causes her. This is relayed in the names that Leah gives her children. She names one son Reuben, in the hope God has "seen" her affliction, so that "now my husband will love me" (ותקרא שמו ראובן כי אמרה כי ראה יהוה בעניי כי עתה יאהבוני אישי, 29:32). The phrase "see my affliction," in verse 32, is typically used in the context of emotional desperation. Here, too, it is not a commentary on disinheritance but a desperate call for her husband to bond with her emotionally. Leah names another son Simeon, hoping that God has "heard" that she was unloved (כי-שמע יהוה כי-שנואה אנכי ויתק-לי גם-את-זה ותקרא שמו שמעון, 29:33). She names a third son Levi, hoping that "now this time my husband will be joined to me because I have borne him three sons" (עתה הפעם ילוה אישי אלי כי-ילדתי לו שלשה בנים על-כן קרא-שמו לוי, 29:34).

The passage juxtaposes the growing desperation of this hated wife against her husband's prosperity; Jacob marries his beloved, Rachel (29:28–30), and is blessed with numerous progenies from both women (Genesis 30). The contrasting descriptions of Jacob's and Leah's conditions casts Jacob's *sn'* over his permanently helpless wife as particularly cruel.

Judges 14–15 offer another instance of spousal *sn'*, the consequences of which, in this passage, are irrevocable. Though in this instance the wife does perpetrate a crime, Samson's wife discloses to the Philistines the solution to his riddle, she is not exactly guilty. Samson's wife is compelled by the Philistines' threat that, were she refuse to betray Samson, they would kill her and her father (14:15).

In response to the betrayal, Samson slaughters Philistines and leaves his wife. Presuming that Samson will not return to his wife whom he hates, his father-in-law marries her to another (ויאמר אמרתי כי-שנא שנאתה ואתננה למרעך אביה אמר, 15:2). When Samson *does* return for his wife, he neither denies hating her nor pursues reconciliation (such as do Abimelech and the elders of Gilead). Instead, he wages an assault against her Philistine kin. The Philistines retaliate by burning her and her father, as they had threatened (16:6). The tragic end of Samson's wife, which is precipitated by her husband's behavior, can be contrasted against Samson's future, which is filled with more women and an illustrious military career. In short, *sn'* is tragic for the vulnerable female target but not for its bearer.

Amnon and Tamar (2 Samuel 13)

2 Samuel 13 describes an exceptionally severe instance of *sn'*, its severity demonstrated in the ways it diverges from the course anticipated by the Female-Targeted *Sn'*-Script. Specifically, the hater is exceptionally iniquitous, the experience of *sn'* is especially intense, and the consequences of *sn'* are extremely damaging.

1. Amnon rapes Tamar.
2. Amnon hates Tamar.
3. Amnon estranges Tamar.
4. Tamar becomes a desolate spinster.

As is anticipated, the hater is the more dominant party who, in this case, physically overpowers a vulnerable woman (13:14–17):

ולא אבה לשמע בקולה ויחזק ממנה ויענה וישכב אתה: וישנאה אמנון שנאה גדולה מאד השנאה אשר שנאה מאהבה אשר אהבה ויאמר-לה אמנון קומי לכי: ותאמר לו אל-אודת הרעה הגדולה הזאת מאחרת אשר-עשית עמי לשלחני ולא אבה לשמע לה: ויקרא את נערו משרתו ויאמר שלחו-נא את-זאת מעלי החוצה ונעל הדלת אחריה:

As we have seen, biblical narratives typically feature an antecedent of *sn'*, which encourages a more benevolent regard for the hater. Laban swindles Jacob and Jacob hates Leah; Jacob favors Joseph and the brothers hate Joseph. The Philistines swindle Samson and Samson hates his wife.

In stark contrast, Amnon hates not because he is mistreated but because of his mistreatment of another. Specifically, Amnon's hate does not cause him to injure Tamar, as would be anticipated. Instead, raping Tamar causes him to hate her. The passage underscores Amnon's singular guilt by using the *hitpa'el* form of חלה to describe how Amnon "causes himself to be sick" (להתחלות) with love.[11]

While Amnon's violation of Tamar is not an act of *sn'*, his refusal to marry her, which is cited immediately thereafter, is (13:16–18). Amnon's repudiation of Tamar is unsurprising, since, as we have seen, an impulse to avoid is a prototypical feature of the idealized model of *sn'*. Even so, the narrator casts Amnon's estrangement of Tamar as especially intense and destructive. Not only does Amnon refuse to marry Tamar, he also sends her out of the room. Not only does Amnon send her out of the room, he also has the door bolted behind her (13:17). Presumably, Amnon could refuse to see Tamar even were he not to secure the door in such a pointedly absolute way. In this context, the bolted door must represent then the intensity with which Amnon seeks to banish his target.

The portrayal of Amnon denying Tamar's entreaty to marry her may reflect an awareness of a law or tradition that enjoins rapists to marry their victims, such as is recorded in Deut 22:28–29. Against the background of this directive, which is likely aimed at protecting women from desolate spinsterhood, Amnon's refusal to marry Tamar is an improper, if not unlawful, repudiation of the liability that he may have incurred by raping her.[12]

Tamar mourns her new status as a desolate woman and lives out her days in Absalom's house. David Tsumura compares Tamar's state of "desolation" to "one who has been [abandoned] or rejected by her husband."[13] Indeed, Tamar expresses her grief and humiliation by tearing her clothes, placing ashes on her head, and crying continually (13:19–20). The narrator underscores the terrible and enduring effect of Amnon's *sn'* on Tamar by juxtaposing it against David's neglect to punish Amnon, in the same passage.[14]

Were 2 Samuel 13 to end at this point, it would conform to the Female-Targeted *Sn'*-Script, according to which the target suffers while her hater thrives. The passage continues, however, with a second account of *sn'*. Absalom hears of Amnon's action, is aroused to *sn'*, and refuses to speak with him—a course of events reminiscent of Amnon's own *sn'* for Tamar (13:21–22):

והמלך דוד שמע את כל-הדברים האלה ויחר לו מאד: ולא-דבר אבשלום עם-אמנון למרע ועד-טוב כי-שנא אבשלום את-אמנון על-דבר אשר ענה את תמר אחתו:

Some commentators argue that Absalom's silence is "duplicitous," since all the while, he hatches a plan to murder his brother.[15] Tsumura rightly argues the contrary; the כי clause, in verse 22, makes it clear that Absalom's *sn'*, as well as its consequent estrangement, is what prevents him from speaking to Amnon. Dominic Rudman explains:

> Yet the כי clause here makes it clear that Absalom's not speaking to his brother is a consequence of his hatred. Absalom's hatred is far from hidden: it is obvious in the fact that he has broken off all social links with his brother. In this context, "to speak neither good nor bad" is probably no more than an idiom meaning "not to speak at all." Absalom's feelings toward Amnon have their parallel in those of Amnon toward Tamar earlier.
>
> (2 Sam 13:1–2)[16]

Absalom's silence recalls the estranged relations between Joseph and his brothers in Genesis 37. When Joseph's brothers hate him, they are unable to speak peaceably to him (37:4). Absalom's silence is more severe, though, for he does not speak to Amnon *at all*. Moreover, Joseph's brothers choose not to kill him, whereas Absalom orders Amnon's murder (2 Sam 13:28).

The reversal of roles, wherein Amnon goes from hating a vulnerable woman to being hated by an older brother, is a divergence from the Female-Targeted *Sn'*-Script that underscores the severity of Amnon's act of *sn'*. Amnon took advantage of his dominance over a woman and suffers dearly for it. Regardless, his death does not restore Tamar's loss; Tamar remains violated and lives out her life supported by Absalom; she is a desolate spinster in his home (13:28).

Legal *Sn'*-Script

Legal texts feature many of the same traits that we find in the Broad Biblical *Sn'*-Script and its narrative variants. The Legal *Sn'*-Script distinguishes itself from the narrative variants, in particular, in underplaying, typically, the antecedents of *sn'*. In biblical narratives, haters target the vulnerable, usually, because they cannot direct *sn'* at more powerful perpetrators. By contrast, in legal texts, haters are not portrayed as victims at all. The *sn'*-script is as follows:

- Subject hates a less powerful and innocent target.
- Subject aims to hurt the target.
- Subject avoids the target.
- Subject achieves no gains.

Examples of *sn'* in legal texts display several traits that overlap with the Broad Biblical *Sn'*-Script. For one, *sn'* is exclusively ascribed to dominant parties who target vulnerable ones.[17] All the cases of marital *sn'* in Deuteronomy describe husbands hating their dependent wives, not the reverse (Deut 21:15; 22:13; 24:3):

כי-תהיין לאיש שתי נשים האחת אהובה והאחת שנואה וילדו-לו בנים האהובה והשנואה והיה הבן הבכר לשניאה: והיה ביום הנחילו את-בניו את אשר-יהיה לו לא יוכל לבכר את-בן-האהובה על-פני בן-השנואה הבכר: כי את-הבכר בן-השנואה יכיר לתת לו פי שנים בכל אשר-ימצא לו כי-הוא ראשית אנו לו משפט הבכרה
21:15–17

כי-יקח איש אשה ובא אליה ושנאה: ושם לה עלילת דברים והוצא עליה שם רע ואמר את-האשה הזאת לקחתי ואקרב אליה ולא-מצאתי לה בתולים:
22:13–14

ושנאה האיש האחרון וכתב לה ספר כריתת ונתן בידה ושלחה מביתו או כי ימות האיש
האחרון אשר-לקחה לו לאשה:
24:3

Second, in all three cases, *sn'* is associated with an urge to harm and/or avoid the target. In Deut 24:3, the hater seeks to divorce his wife. In Deut 22:13–14, the hater spuriously accuses his wife of a crime whose conviction would result in her execution. And Deut 21:15–16 presumes that a hater would cheat his wife's progeny out of his legitimate inheritance.

A number of scholars maintain that in marital texts, *sn'* has a performative function as a technical term for divorce.[18] In fact, Riley argues that in none of these legal cases does *sn'* connote an intense emotional experience. Rather, *sn'* in Deut 21:15–17 is "a metaphor for marital demotion and not a lexeme with an intense emotional overtone." For him, the passage that enjoins against cheating the son of a hated wife out of his inheritance designates a moderate level of emotion that conveys less affection or neglect toward the wife. As evidence, he points out that the husband must have had sexual relations with his "hated" wife in order to conceive a son.[19] This presumption, however—that sexual relations preclude *sn'*—seems a bit overreaching and anachronistic.

Riley argues, as well, that *sn'* conveys only a moderate degree of emotion and connotes a more strongly technical demotion in marital status in Deut 22:13–15. Yet the hater seeks to have his wife executed on false grounds, which suggests an intense urge to harm. In fact, *sn'* is associated with an urge to harm in virtually all *sn'* passages in legal texts. Even the single law associated with *sn'* in Exodus enjoins a hater to help his targets' donkeys, which indicates that haters were not inclined to assist those whom they hate (Exod 23:5):

כי-תראה חמור שנאך רבץ תחת משאו וחדלת מעזב לו עזב תעזב עמו:

Wherever exactly *sn'* falls on an affective spectrum, the thrust of these passages is not on the triggering offense, but that *sn'* comes with both an urge to harm and estrange.[20]

Moreover, none of the cases of spousal *sn'* in Deuteronomy offers any explanation for *why* husbands hate their wives and neither do the descriptions of haters committing premeditated murder. The closest a verse comes to offering an explanation is Deuteronomy 22 statement that a husband hates his wife immediately after he has sex with her. The sequence implies that unsatisfying sex is the antecedent of *sn'* and not the wife's willful transgression. In underplaying the antecedent of *sn'*, the legal *sn'*-script offers a more robust condemnation of the emotion than does the narrative *sn'*-script.

Notes

1. Examples of *sn'* in biblical narratives tend to bear a stronger family resemblance to the Male- and Female-Targeted *Sn'*-Scripts than to the Broad-Biblical *Sn'*-Script because they all are members of the same narrower category.
2. While the term נער can mean "young male," anywhere between the ages of infancy and young adulthood, it may also refer to the subservient role of a servant. The latter connotation would underscore Joseph's particularly humble role as subservient to the sons of Jacob's concubines. Victor H. Matthews, "The Anthropology of Clothing in the Joseph Narrative," *Journal for Study of Old Testament* 20/65 (1995): 29–35.
3. The bestowal and removal of attire is a well-known theme in cultural studies, signifying a change in social standing; Victor Matthews, "The Anthropology of Clothing within the Joseph Narrative," 31–32.
4. Claus Westermann, *Genesis 37–50*, trans. John J. Scullion (Minneapolis: Augsburg, 1986), 37.
5. The stripping of this garment represents Joseph's "descending status from favored son to slave"; Kenneth Mathews, *Genesis 11:27–50:26* (Nashville: Broadman and Holman, 2005), 685–89. See also Matthews, "The Anthropology of Clothing," 31; Westermann, *Genesis 37–50*, 37.
6. See Mathews, *Genesis 11:27–50:26*, 685.
7. On the meaning of "elders," see Klaas Spronk, *Historical Commentary of the Old Testament: Judges* (Leuven: Peeters, 2019), 331.
8. On the identity of Jephthah's mother, see Spronk, *Historical Commentary of the Old Testament*, 331.
9. While they worry that he has become too powerful (26:16), it appears that he is not yet powerful enough to oppose them.
10. Szubin and Porten, "The Status of a Repudiated Spouse: A New Interpretation of Kraeling 7 (TAD B3.8)," *Israel Law Review* (2001): 58–59.
11. Typically, love is the inverse of hate: love generates well-being, whereas hate causes injury. In this instance, though, Amnon's "sickening love" compels him to harm his beloved (ויאהבה...ויצר לאמנון להתחלות, 13:1–2); Gerhard Wallis, Jan Bergman, and A. O. Haldar, "אהב *'āhabh*," *TDOT* 1:104–12.
12. Biblical law states that if a man seduces or rapes an unmarried or unbetrothed woman, he must marry her (unless her father refuses), and he is not permitted to divorce her. The tradition is likely intended to protect the woman from desolate spinsterhood and repay her immediate family. In the ancient world, "all sex between a man and the female ward of non-consenting male guardians" is "akin to theft of property." William Propp, "Kinship in 2 Samuel 13," *Catholic Biblical Quarterly* 55 (1993): 41. Amnon *stole* David's daughter and refuses to repay his debt. David, however, is unwilling to punish the violation against the family, likely because Amnon is his son, and so Absalom takes it upon himself to do so (13:21). Tamar refers to the violation as a נבלה בישראל, which is the same phrase that Dinah's brothers use to describe Shechem's violation of Dinah in Genesis 34, as well as Achan's theft of sacred utensils in Joshua 7.
13. Tsumura remarks on the infinitive of emphasis ותלך הלוך, translating it literally as, "and went continually and cried"; David Toshio Tsumura, *The Second Book of Samuel* (Grand Rapids: Eerdmans, 2019), 209. See Isa 49:8; 54:1.
14. 1 Sam 13:21.
15. See, for example, Phyllis Trible, *Texts of Terror: Literary-Feminist Readings of Biblical Narratives* (Minneapolis: Fortress, 1984), 51.

16 Dominic Rudman, "Reliving the Rape of Tamar: Absalom's Revenge in 2 Samuel 13," *Old Testament Essays* 1 (1998): 330.
17 See also Deut 4:42; 19:6, 11; Josh 20:5.
18 See discussion in Delbert R. Hillers, "Some Performative Utterances in the Bible," in idem, *Poets before Homer: Collected Essays on Ancient Literature*, ed. F. W. Dobbs-Allsopp (Winona Lake: Eisenbrauns, 2015), 301n22.
19 Riley, *Divine and Human Hate in Ancient Near East* (Piscataway: Gorgias Press, 2017), 27–29.
20 *Sn'* precipitates premeditated murder in other legal passages as well, such as Deut 19:11; see also Deut 4:42; 19:14; Josh 20:5.

5 Poetic and Prophetic *Sn'*-Scripts

Research psychologist James Russell reminds us that emotion-scripts are embedded in networks of related concepts.[1] It is not surprising, then, that the themes of divine dominance and divine justice, which suffuse poetic and prophetic texts, are central to Old Poetic and prophetic *sn'*-scripts.

We discern three prominent variants of the Broad Biblical *Sn'*-Script in Old Poetic and prophetic texts. They are the God-Targeted *Sn'*-Script, the Evil-Targeted *Sn'*-Script, and the Divine *Sn'*-Script. The scripts overlap with the broader model of *sn'* in their characterizations of haters as powerful persecutors of their targets. However, they diverge from the course of *sn'* anticipated by the Broad Biblical *Sn'*-Script in order to portray God as more powerful or more righteous than human beings; haters succumb, rather than dominate their target, and *sn'* is a response to injustice and sin, not the cause of it.

Identifying the Old Poetic and prophetic variants helps us to discern the unique tenor of *sn'* in individual passages.

God-Targeted *Sn'*-Script (in Poetic Texts)

The God-Targeted *Sn'*-Script overlaps with the idealized model of *sn'* represented by the Broad-Biblical *Sn'*-Script in some ways and diverges from it in others. The script is as follows:

- Subject hates God or God's followers.
- Subject harms God or God's followers.
- God harms or God's followers harm the subject.

As anticipated by the broader model, the God-Targeted *Sn'*-Script features powerful haters who come in great numbers and with strong might:

יצילני מאיבי עז משנאי כי אמצו ממני:
2 Sam 22:18

DOI: 10.4324/9781003348719-5

ראה-איבי כי-רבו ושנאת חמס שנאוני:
Ps 25:19

רבו משערות ראשי שנאי חנם עצמו מצמיתי איבי שקר אשר לא-גזלתי אז אשיב:
Ps 69:5

The God-Targeted *Sn'*-Script overlaps with the Broad-Biblical *Sn'*-Script also in featuring innocent targets. Some poetic passages even claim that *sn'* arises for no reason whatsoever:

אל-ישמחו-לי איבי שקר שנאי חנם יקרצו-עין:
Ps 35:19

ואיבי חיים עצמו שנאי שקר:
Ps 38:19

רבו משערות ראשי שנאי חנם עצמו מצמיתי איבי שקר אשר לא-גזלתי אז אשיב:
Ps 69:5

Throughout biblical poetry, haters are frequently identified as God's enemies (צר or אויב):

ויהי בנסע הארן ויאמר משה קומה יהוה ויפצו איביך וינסו משנאיך מפניך:
Num 10:35

אם-שנותי ברק חרבי ותאחז במשפט ידי אשיב נקם לצרי ולמשנאי אשלם:
Deut 32:41

ברך יהוה חילו ופעל ידיו תרצה מחץ מתנים קמיו ומשנאיו מן-יקומון:
Deut 33:11

תמצא ידך לכל-איביך ימינך תמצא שנאיך ... פרימו מארץ תאבד וזרעם מבני אדם ... כי תשיתמו שכם במיתריך תכונן על-פניהם:
Ps 21:9–12

יקום אלהים יפוצו אויביו וינסו משנאיו מפניו:
Ps 68:1

While the identities of God's many enemies remain obscure, what is clear is that they are one and the same as his haters.[2]

As is distinct from the broader model of *sn'*, which features powerful haters harming vulnerable targets, God's haters succumb to their target. The portrayal of God overpowering and grievously harming his haters—a deviation from the anticipated course of *sn'*—underscores God's exceptional dominance. In fact, when we approach the Psalms as a single corpus, God's dominance emerges in clear relief and by way of contrast. Haters typically seek to harm their targets:

כי-דרש דמים אותם זכר לא-שכח צעקת ענייִם:
Ps 9:13

ראה-איבי כי-רבו ושנאת חמס שנאת:
Ps 25:19

יחד עלי יתלחשו כל-שנאי עלי יחשבו רעה לי:
Ps 41:8

כי לא-אויב יחרפני ואשא לא-משנאי עלי הגדיל ואסתר ממנו:
Ps 55:13

רבו משערות ראשי שנאי חנם עצמו מצמיתי איבי שקר אשר לא-גזלתי אז אשיב:
Ps 69:5

But when God is the target, the haters are harmed instead:

כי לא-אויב יחרפני ואשא לא-משנאי עלי הגדיל ואסתר ממנו:
Ps 55:13

בך צרינו ננגח בשמך נבוס קמינו: כי לא בקשתי אבטח וחרבי לא תושיענו: כי הושעתנו מצרינו ומשנאינו הבישות:
Ps 44:6–8

ישלח ממרום יקחני ימשני ממים רבים: יצליני מאיבי עז ומשנאי כי-אמצו ממני... ותאזרני חיל למלחמה תכריע קמי תחתי: ואיבי נתתה לי ערף ומשנאי אצמיתם:
Ps 18:17–18, 40–41[3]

Evil-Targeted *Sn'*-Script (in Poetic Texts)

Throughout the Bible, a stark dichotomy is drawn between the righteous, who accept God's sovereignty, and the wicked, who do not. Often, this dichotomy is expressed through the language of *'hb* and *sn'*; those who are righteous love God and abide in his ways, and those who are wicked hate him and do not abide in his ways. Thus, we read in the Ten Commandments (Deut 9:9–10):

לא-תשתחוה להם ולא תעבדם כי אנכי יהוה אלהיך אל קנא פקד עון אבות על-בנים ועל-שלשים ועל-רבעים לשנאי: ועשה חסד לאלפים לאהבי ולשמרי מצותו:

In the Psalms, in particular, the line between loving and hating God lies at one's orientation toward social justice (less so than on worship).[4]

Those who love God eschew social injustice and those who hate God engage in it. The theme forms a distinct *sn'*-script, which we refer to as the Evil-Targeted *Sn'*-Script:

- Subject hates the wicked target.
- Subject estranges the wicked target.
- Subject is supported by God.

Sn' and social justice are paired, in this script, in a starkly different way from how they are associated in the rest of the Bible. Although the idealized model associates *sn'* with cruel and unjust harm to the vulnerable and innocent, this variant-script portrays *sn'* as a response to social injustice and not the cause:[5]

לא-ישבתי עם-מתי-שוא ועם נעלמים לא אבוא: שנאתי קהל מרעים ועם נעלמים לא אבוא: שנאתי קהל מרעים ועם-רשעים לא אשב: ארחץ בנקיון כפי ואסבבה את-מזבחך יהוה: לשמע בקול תודה ולספר כל-נפלאותיך: יהוה אהבתי מעון ביתך ומקום משכן כבודך: אל-תאסף עם-חטאים נפשי ועם-אנשי דמים חיי:
Ps 26:4–9

סעפים שנאתי ותורתך אהבתי:
Ps 119:13

על-כן אהבתי מצותיך מזהב ומפז: על-כן כל-פקודי כל ישרתי כל-ארח שקר שנאתי:
Ps 119:127–28

כסאך אלהים עולם ועד שבט מישר שבט מלכותך: אהבת צדק ותשנא-רשע על-כן משחך אלהים אלהיך שמן ששון מחברך:
Ps 45:8

Haters distance themselves from their targets, as is anticipated by the idealized model, but in this variant, avoidance is a righteous act:

לא-ישבתי עם-מתי-שוא ועם נעלמים לא אבוא: שנאתי קהל מרעים ועם-רשעים לא אשב:
Ps 26:4–5

לא-אשית לנגד עיני דבר-בליעל עשה-סטים שנאתי לא ידבק בי:
Ps 101:3[6]

Divine *Sn'*-Script

Biblical passages that portray God-hating are rare, but when they do show up, they share a common script. As this script is attested across various biblical collections, its features are shaped, more likely, by the subject's divinity than by literary setting. The script is as follows:

- God hates the guilty target.
- God estranges the target.
- God harms the target.

Resembling the Broad-Biblical Sn'-Script

Current studies from the fields of psychology and religion posit that anthropomorphic language highlights both God's likenesses to *and* God's differences from what is not divine.[7] In this vein, some elements of God's *sn'* resemble *sn'*-scripts elsewhere in the Hebrew Bible, while other elements are distinct. In accord with the idealized model of *sn'*, God is always the more dominant party, his *sn'* is typically precipitated by offense, and it is usually associated with harm.

God harms the targets of his *sn'* in various ways, such as delivering them to the hands of their enemies, making their lands a desolation, and raining fire down upon them:

כל-רעתם בגלגל כי-שם שנאתים על רע מעלליהם מביתי אגרשם לא אוסף אהבתם
כל-שריהם סררים: הכה אפרים שרשם יבש פרי בל יעשון גם כי ילדון והמתי מחמדי
בטנם: ימאסם אלהי כי לא שמעו לו ויהיו נדדים בגוים:
Hos 9:15–17

יהוה צדיק יבחן ורשע ואהב חמס שנאה נפשו: ימטר על-רשעים פחים אש וגפרית ורוח
זלעפות מנת כוסם:
Ps 11:6

ואת-עשו שנאתי ואשים את-הריו שממה ואת-נחלתו לתנות מדבר:
Mal 1:3

נשבע אדני יהוה בנפשו נאם-יהוה אלהי צבאות מתאב אנכי את-גאון יעקב וארמנתיו
שנאתי והסגרתי עיר ומלאה: והיה אם-יותרו עשרה אנשים בבית אחד ומתו:
Amos 6:8–9

Also in accord with the Broad-Biblical *Sn'*-Script, God avoids his targets, driving them from his house and abandoning them:[8]

כל-רעתם בגלגל כי-שם שנאתים על רע מעלליהם מביתי אגרשם לא אוסף אהבתם
כל-שריהם סררים: הכה אפרים שרשם יבש פרי בל יעשון גם ילדון והמתי מחמדי בטנם:
ימאסם אלהי כי לא שמעו לו ויהיו נדדים בגוים:
Hos 9:15–17

עזבתי את-ביתי נטשתי את-נחלתי נתתי את-ידדות נפשי בכף איביה: היתה-לי נחלתי
כאריה ביער נתנה עלי בקולה על-כן שנאתיה:
Jer 12:7–8

The anthropopathic rendering of God as possessing emotions encourages an empathetic regard, which both Amos and Isaiah leverage to explain why God abandons his people. Amos warns (5:21–24):

שנאתי מאסתי חגיכם ולא אריח בעצרתיכם: כי אם-תעלו-לי עלות ומנחתיכם לא ארצה
ושלם מריאיכם לא אביט: הסר מעלי המון שריך וזמרת נבליך לא אשמע: ויגל כמים משפט
וצדקה כנחל איתן:

In keeping with the idealized model of *sn'*, God is compelled to abandon his people because he cannot bear their worship. Indeed, human haters cannot bear the presence of their targets as well, even when they are otherwise expected to do so. Instead of marrying Tamar, Amnon sends her away. Instead of divvying up inheritance equitably, Jephthah's brothers exile him. Instead of speaking with Joseph, his brothers leave him in a pit.

Amos extends the anthropomorphic theme more broadly, ascribing to God not only an emotion but also a human body that must bear this emotion. The angry God refuses to *smell* (with his nose) or *look* (with his eyes) at Israel's offerings, or to *listen* (with his ears) to their songs.[9] Göran Eidevall compares God's reaction to the reaction of someone who wants to cancel a relationship. It is as if God is saying, "I don't want your presents, I don't want to see you! I can't stand listening to your voice!"[10] *Sn'* compels God to keep his distance, which leaves his people vulnerable to attack (5:26–27).

Isaiah makes explicit what is implicit in Amos—the vulnerability of a God who possesses both human emotions and a human body; as would be human beings, God is *wearied* of carrying his people's burden (1:11–15):

למה-לי רב-זבחיכם יאמר יהוה שבעתי עלות אילים וחלב מריאים ודם פרים וכבשים
ועתודים לא חפצתי: כי תבאו לראות פני מי- בקש זאת מידכם רמס חצרי: לא תוסיפו
הביא מנחת-שוא קטרת תועבה היא לי חדש ושבת קרא מקרא לא-אוכל ועצרה: חדשיכם
ומועדיכם שנאה נפשי היו עלי לטרח נלאיתי נשא: ובפרשכם כפיכם אעלים עיני מכם גם
כי-תרבו תפלה אינני שמע ידיכם דמים מלאו:

When the phrase שנאה נפשי is paired with לאה (here in the phrase נלאיתי נשא), the latter may refer to a tendency to be overwhelmed by emotions, even to one's own detriment.[11] In his weariness, God *hides his eyes* from his people, refuses to *listen* to their songs, and *hates* their worship; he is unable, or at least unwilling, to bear the distress associated with *sn'*. The anthropomorphism thus explains that God may abandon his people because he is not impervious to the suffering they cause him.

Distinctly Divine Sn'

Guilty Targets

As we have seen, the conceptual model of *sn'*, as represented in the Broad-Biblical *Sn'*-Script, has haters targeting vulnerable and innocent parties. By contrast, the Divine *Sn'*-Script has God targeting the guilty. Typically, God's targets are guilty of social injustices like murder and violence. Thus, we read in the Psalms:

כי לא אל-חפץ רשע אתה לא יגרך רע: לא-יתיצבו הוללים לנגד עיניך שנאתי כל-פעלי און:
תאבד דברי כזב איש-דמים ומרמה יתעב יהוה:
Ps 5:5–7

יהוה צדיק יבחן ורשע ואהב חמס שנאה נפשו:
Ps 11:5

Even Amos 5, which implies that illegitimate worship is the precipitator of God's *sn'*, signals that the real source of it is social injustice (5:10–24):[12]

שנאו בשער מוכיח ודבר תמים יתעבו: לכן יען בושסכם על-דל ומשאת-בר תקחו ממנו
בתי גזית בניתם: ולא-תשבו בם כרמי-חמד נטעתם ולא תשתו את-יינם: כי ידעתי רבים
פשעיכם ועצמים חטאתיכם צררי צדיק לקחי כפר ואביונים בשער הטו: לכן המשכיל בעת
ההיא ידם כי עת רעה היא: דרשו-טוב ואל-רע למען תחיו ויהי-כן יהוה אלהי-צבאות אתכם
כאשר אמרתם: שנאו-רע ואהבו טוב והציגו בשער משפט אולי יחנן יהוה אלהי-צבאות
שארית יוסף: לכן כה-אמר יהוה אלהי צבאות אדני בכל-רחבת מספד ובכל-חוצות יאמרו
הו-הו וקראו אכר אל-אבל ומספד אל-יודעי נהי: ובכל-כרמים מספד כי-אעבר בקרבך אמר
יהוה: הוי המתאוים את-יום יהוה למה-זה לכם יום יהוה הוא-חשך ולא-אור: כאשר ינוס
איש מפני הארי ופגעו הדב ובא הבית וסמך ידו על-הקיר ונשכו הנחש: הלא-חשך יום יהוה
ולא-אור ואפל ולא-נגה לו: שנאתי מאסתי חגיכם ולא אריח בעצרתיכם: כי אם-תעלו-לי
עלות ומנחתיכם לא ארצה ושלם מריאכם לא אביט: הסר מעלי המון שריך
וזמרת נבליך לא אשמע: ויגל כמים משפט וצדקה כנחל איתן:

In this passage, *sn'* is the linchpin that connects God's rejection of Israel to the people's cruel and unjust practices. The passage recounts how corrupt sinners trample on and steal from the poor, afflict the righteous, take bribes, and push aside the needy, and also how they hate those who rebuke them for it.[13] Shortly thereafter, the passage declares that God hates Israel's festivals and sacrifices. The juxtaposition of these two references to *sn'*—sinners' hate and God's hate—indicates that they are related; when the wicked hate their rebukers, God shuns the wicked—specifically, by hating the sacrifices that would otherwise maintain his relationship with them.[14]

A long-standing theological discomfort with the idea that God hates may account for the robust discussion around Mal 1:2. The passage, which states that God hates Esau, is the only instance in the Hebrew Bible where God hates a named person (1:2–5):

אהבתי אתכם אמר יהוה ואמרתם במה אהבתנו הלוא-אח עשו ליעקב נאם-יהוה ואהב את-יעקב: ואת-עשו שנאתי ואשים את-הריו שממה ואת-נחלתו לתנות מדבר: כי-תאמר אדום רששנו ונשוב ונבנה חרבות כה אמר יהוה צבאות המה יבנו ואני אהרוס וקראו להם גבול רשעה והעם אשר-זעם יהוה עד-עולם: ועיניכם תראינה ואתם תאמרו יגדל יהוה מעל לגבול ישראל:

Some argue that "the use of so strong a verb as *sn'*" is a result of "the scarcity of adjectives in Hebrew." Others contend that "not too much should be made of Yahweh's hate for Esau/Edom in this pericope."[15] A number of scholars suggest that the terms "love" and "hate" in this passage do not connote feelings but rather actions that mean "prefer" and "not prefer" or "elect" and "reject." God's *sn'* for Esau thus reflects a "relative difference in God's feelings toward his sons," whereby one is chosen for the covenant and the other is not. As is similarly argued, "Yahweh affirms that he has shown love for Israel by his choice of Jacob/Israel rather than Esau/Edom."[16]

Typically, love compels people to help their beloved and *sn'* compels people to harm them. Israel's question to God presumes as much. When Israel asks, "How have you loved us?" the people are really asking, "What is the proof of your love for us when our enemy thrives?" God responds by asserting that even though Esau is Jacob's brother and a descendant of Abraham (the same as Jacob), God acts in love to help Israel by acting in *sn'* to harm her enemy.[17]

Recognizing the sequence of traits anticipated by the Broad Biblical *Sn'*-Script, permits us to better understand the thrust of Moses' intercession at Horeb. When God threatens to destroy the people because they have sinned with the golden calf, Moses successfully appeals their case (Deut 9:25–29):

ואתנפל לפני יהוה את ארבעים היום ואת-ארבעים הלילה אשר התנפלתי כי-אמר יהוה להשמיד אתכם: ואתפלל אל-יהוה ואמר אדני יהוה אל-תשחת עמך ונחלך אשר פדית בגדלך אשר-הוצאת ממצרים ביד חזקה: זכר לעבדיך לאברהם ליצחק וליעקב אל-תפן אל-קשי העם הזה ואל-רשעו ואל-חטאתו: פן-יאמרו הארץ אשר הוצאתנו מבלי יכלת יהוה להביאם אל-הארץ אשר-דבר להם ומשנאתו אותם הוציאם להמיתם במדבר: והם עמך ונחלתך אשר הוצאת בכחך הגדל ובזרע הנטויה:

Moses begins his appeal not by arguing that Israel's sin is modest but by evoking the patriarchs. Scholars often suggest that by bringing up the patriarchs, Moses is requesting God to act in accord with the covenant oath he made to them, which is to protect and bless their progeny in the Land of Israel.

While this may be the case, Moses does not seem confident that his appeal to the covenant is, on its own, enough to prevent God from annihilating the people. Instead, Moses persists with additional arguments that revolve around God's reputation. First, Moses warns God that, were he to destroy his people, the world would think him *unable* to bring them to the Land of Israel; God's reputation as a powerful deity who redeemed his people with signs and wonders is at stake.[18]

Thereafter, Moses argues that were God to kill the people of Israel, others might think, "because he hated them, he has brought them out to let them die in the wilderness" (9:28). Richard Nelson and Riley, among others, see this appeal to God's reputation as wrapped up with Moses' former appeals. Moses is warning that "some might think that Yahweh was an ineffective God, whose relationship to the people was a deceitful one of hostility under the guise of promise."[19] As Riley understands it, Moses is warning that God may be perceived as disloyal to his own covenant.[20]

We interpret the verses differently. It seems clear that Moses' second warning relates to God's reputation as competent (הוצאתנו מבלי יכלת יהוה להביאם אל-הארץ אשר-דבר להם). Moses' third warning, however, which accuses God of *sn'*, relates to his reputation as just (ומשנאתו אותם הוציאם להמיתם במדבר). As we know, a central trait of *sn'* is the harm it causes to innocent targets. Moses is cautioning God that, were he to kill his people, he would be viewed akin to a prototypical hater who unjustly harms the vulnerable and innocent.[21]

Conceptual Transfer: Hating Objects, Conduct, and Body Parts[22]

The Divine *Sn'*-Script distinguishes itself in its recurring use of metonymy as a way to underscore the unique justness of God's *sn'*. Inanimate objects, abstract conduct, and body parts are all expressed targets of God's *sn'*. But they are not the intended targets. They are, rather, stand-ins for the people who use, perform, and possess them. Substituting the sinners for their own objects, conduct, and body parts focuses attention on the sinners' identities, insofar as they are purveyors of sin, leaving other aspects of their character and behavior indistinct. The message is that, unlike human haters, God hates only the guilty and for no other reason than that they are guilty.

Deuteronomy 16 offers an example of this with its description of God hating an inanimate object. The language is jarring, since *sn'* is typically directed at people (16:22):

ולא-תקים לך מצבה אשר שנא יהוה אלהיך[23]

In the context of illegitimate worship, the standing stone and the human worshiper are closely related concepts: the standing stone is an instrument and the worshiper is its user. By allowing the illegitimate object to "stand for" the person who worships it, the verse directs attention to the human worshiper only insofar as he is conceptually related to his sin.[24] In this way, the verse discourages any hint that God's *sn'* is unjust. God hates the guilty for no other reason than that they are guilty.

A similar conceptual transfer is evident in descriptions of God hating social injustice. For example, Zechariah 8 and Isaiah 61 declare that God hates "the thinking of evil thoughts," "false oaths," "robbery," and "violence":

ואיש את-רעהו אל-תחשבו בלבבכם ושבעת שקר אל-אתהבו כי את-כל-אלה אשר שנאתי
נאם-יהוה
Zech 8:17

כי אני יהוה אהב משפט שנא גזל בעולה ונתתי פעלתם באמת וברית עולם אכרת להם
Isa 61:8

In each instance, *products* or *actions* stand for the people who *do* or *produce* them. By directing God's *sn'*, literally, at unjust behaviors instead of at the people who perform them, the verses direct attention to the human worshipers only insofar as they are conceptually related to their sinful practices.

In a final example of this literary device, Proverbs 6 conjures the image of a body, by listing the body's disparate parts in vertical order:

שש-הנה שנא יהוה ושבע תועבות נפשו: עינים רמות לשון שקר וידים שפכת דם-נקי:
לב חרש מחשבות און רגלים ממהרות לרוץ לרעה: יפיח כזבים עד שקר ומשלח מדנים
בין אחים

Bernd Heine, among others, points out that "the human body provides one of the most salient models for understanding, describing, and denoting concepts that are more difficult to understand, describe, and denote": "Body parts are visible and tangible objects that are always available to speakers in day-to-day communication. As such, they provide an ideal template for understanding and expressing concepts that are non-visible and non-tangible."[25] Heine explains: "Certain body parts tend to be associated with specific human activities. The cognitive process concerned appears to be one where the use of the body part term is extended metonymically to express the activity typically carried out by or involving the relevant body part."[26]

Each body part cited in Proverbs 6—eyes, tongue, hand, heart, and feet—stands for the person as a whole and is used idiomatically to convey an abstract social interaction. The term "tongue," in the phrase "lying tongue," represents the person who possesses the tongue. The term "lying" in this phrase directs attention to the tongue's function as a vehicle of speech—specifically, speech that constitutes lies. Similarly, in the phrase "bloody hands" (more literally, "hands of poured, innocent blood"), the term "hands" stands for the person who possesses them. The phrase "poured innocent blood" stands for the act of murder that is performed by these hands and that results in the discharge of blood from an innocent body.

In short, by substituting the whole persons who commit sins with the body parts that literally execute them, Proverbs compels us to regard the targets of God's *sn'* only insofar as they are sinners.[27]

Excursus—The Case of Divorce: Misreading Mal 2:16

Another behavior that God is said to hate is divorce. Mal 2:16 reads:

כי-שנא שלח אמר יהוה אלהי ישראל וכסה חמס על-לבושו אמר יהוה צבאות ונשמרתם
ברוחכם ולא תבגדו:

Many interpreters have doubted the plain reading of this passage. Scholars make statements such as: it is "impossible that the verse refers to literal divorce," "the outright rejection of divorce by YHWH formulated in a wholly general way would be astonishing," "it must be sincerely doubted whether in Old Testament times even a prophet would have denounced divorce as a crime," and "'for I hate divorce' must be dismissed for reasons of logic."[28]

A common argument against the plain reading of this verse is that divorce does not seem like a severe injustice on the level of the other behaviors that God hates, such as violence, robbery, and bloodshed. It is argued, as well, that since Malachi is highly influenced by the Deuteronomic perspective, it unlikely that the prophet would prohibit divorce when Deuteronomy permits it.[29]

An alternative suggestion is to interpret the verse figuratively. In this vein, one scholar proposes that verse 16 is "an attack against apostasy to an alien cult that has nothing to do with literal marriage and divorce."[30] Proponents of this position point out that, contextually, much of the rest of Malachi is interested in cultic and priestly matters, not interpersonal relations. Others suggest that the verse should be interpreted literally, but more narrowly, as condemning the practice of divorcing Jewish wives in order to marry gentile women.[31]

Gordon Hugenberger offers a compelling interpretation of Mal 2:16 that retains the literal meaning of the verse and is also consistent with Deuteronomy. He translates: "If one hates and divorces, says

Yahweh, God of Israel, he covers his garment with violence, says Yahweh of hosts." According to this translation—which interprets כי as the unmarked conditional "if" and ו (in וכסה) as the apodosis "then"—the verse describes human *sn'*, not divine *sn'*. This interpretation stands on the fact that, syntactically, God is not the explicit subject of *sn'*. Perhaps, then, Malachi is not arguing that God hates divorce. He is arguing, rather, that God views a divorce that is founded on *sn'* as akin to violence. Hugenberger explains, "While Malachi says nothing to imply that such divorces were illegal, he does condemn divorce based on aversion as ethically reprehensible and as an instance of infidelity [בגד], or covenant breaking (cf. 2:14) susceptible to divine judgment."[32] Hugenberger points out that this reading accords nicely with Deut 24:1–4, which presupposes a negative appraisal of *sn'*-based divorce but nonetheless allows it.

Hugenberger's reading accords nicely, as well, with the Legal *Sn'*-Script. Each case of spousal *sn'* in Deuteronomy involves a concomitant act of injustice against the wife. Husbands who divorce their hated wives also steal from them, accuse them falsely, and commit violence against them. Deuteronomy's association of spousal *sn'* with injustice suggests that Hugenberger's reading of the verse is correct with one qualification: it is not the divorce that is indefensible; it is the violent injustice that invariably accompanies *sn'*-based divorce, which is inexcusable.

Notably, the three injustices that divorcing men inflict on their wives in Deuteronomy—theft, false accusation, and violence—are the same injustices that God is said to hate in the Prophets and Proverbs. Were we to read Mal 1:16 against the backdrop of divine *sn'*, we may interpret it, in fact, as offering an example of the kind of social injustice that God hates.[33]

Notes

1 For summaries of prophetic and poetic themes, see Marvin Sweeney, *The Prophetic Literature* (Nashville: Abingdon, 2005); William Brown, *Psalms* (Nashville: Abingdon, 2010). See also Russell and Fehr, "Fuzzy Concepts in a Fuzzy Hierarchy: Varieties of Anger," *Journal of Personality and Social Psychology* 67 (1994): 202.

2 In some cases, "enemies" refers to various political adversaries of Israel; in other cases, it refers to personal persecutors of the petitioner. For a summary of positions, see Martin J. Slabbert, "Coping in a Harsh Reality: The Concept of the 'Enemy' in the Compositions of Psalms 9 and 10," *HTS Theological Studies* 71/3 (2015): n. 1. It is possible that "the poet deliberately doesn't want to ascribe a stable and identifiable identity to the 'enemy,' so that they remain paradigmatic 'enemies of the people' and their God". Slabbert theorizes: "The enemy is an essential villain to help create and reinforce this positive image of the righteous," 2, 3.

3 God's dominance over haters is described in a number of different ways across poetry and prophetic literature. God compels his haters to scatter

or flee (Num 10:35; 2 Sam 22:18, 41; Pss 18:41; 68:2); he smites or wipes them out (Gen 24:16; Deut 32:41; 33:11; 2 Sam 22:18; Pss 18:41 21:9; 89:24; 118:17); they cower (Ps 81:6); they are shamed (Pss Job 8:22; 86:19; 129:25); they are triumphed over (2 Sam 22:18; Job 8:22; Pss 81:16; 86:17; 118:7); 129:25).

4 See also Ps 34:21; 50:17; Job 8:22.
5 See also Ps 97:10; 101:1–3.
6 The Psalms also attest many examples of the righteous hating the wicked: Pss 5:6; 11:5; 26:5; 31:7; 36:3; 45:8; 97:10; 101:3; 119:104, 113, 128, 163.
7 Paul and Suzanne Mallery and Richard Gorsuch observe that people perceive God as having different, but not necessarily opposite, qualities than humans. "A Preliminary Taxonomy of Attributions to God," *The International Journal for the Psychology of Religion* 10/3 (2000): 135–56.
8 See also Deut 1:12; 9:28; Ps 5:5.
9 מאס has a broad semantic range; one usage connotes a person's contempt for another party, such as a husband's contempt for his wife (Isa 54:6). S. Wagner, "מאס *māʾas*," *Theological Dictionary of the Old Testament* 8:49, 55. Early classical prophecy also features strong emotional components of מאס, such as Amos 5:21.
10 Göran Eidevall, "Rejected Sacrifice in the Prophetic Literature: A Rhetorical Perspective," *Svensk Exegetisk Årsbok* 78 (2013): 42.
11 The root לאה connotes exhaustion from carrying a burden; see Isa 7:13.
12 Isa 1:11–15 offers another example of this. In the past, some have interpreted these passages as an appeal to relate to God in a new, "more abstract," way, or to focus on ethical conduct over cultic worship. Others have suggested that the passage demands a wholesale rejection of cultic worship. Yet, as Eidevall, among others, points out, the Pentateuch is replete with commands and instruction about how to worship God cultically. This makes it unlikely that the passage argues for the rejection of cultic worship altogether. It is more likely that Amos rejects worship not accompanied by social injustice. For a summary of opinions, see Göran Eidevall, *Amos: A New Translation with Introduction and Commentary* (New Haven: Yale University Press, 2017), 166–67.
13 Whether the context is immediately prior to, or immediately after, the fall of Samaria, it was likely taken as evidence that God was abandoning his people.
14 As Eidevall understands it, Amos 5 claims that the sacrificial cult is a self-perpetuating gift from God. It is a mechanism whereby Israel can give gifts *to* God in order to maintain their relationship with him. Unfortunately, the people's rampant social injustice has rendered God's gift ineffective; the cult no longer upholds Israel's relationship with God. With no means to repent and to be heard, the people of Israel are doomed; Eidevall, "Rejected Sacrifice," 42.
15 Paul L. Redditt, "The God Who Loves and Hates," in *Shall Not the Judge of All the Earth Do What Is Right? Studies on the Nature of God in Tribute to James L. Crenshaw*, ed. David Penchansky and Paul L. Redditt (Winona Lake: Eisenbrauns, 2000), 176, 178.
16 Redditt, "The God Who Loves and Hates," 176.
17 While Malachi does not explicitly describe Esau as guilty, the Bible does identify Esau with Edomites, who are guilty of barring Israel's crossing upon leaving Egypt. See Gen 36:1; Deut 2:12; Num 20:14–21. Esau comes to be paradigmatic of many enemies of Israel. For a summary of late antiquity and rabbinic sources conflating Esau with Edom and Rome, see Malka Simkovich, "Esau the Ancestor of Rome," thetorah.com.ץ

18 The book of Exodus similarly claims that God's wondrous redemption of Israel and attendant destruction of Egypt are aimed at demonstrating God's great power throughout the land; see Exod 9:14–16; 13:17.
19 Richard Nelson, *Deuteronomy: A Commentary* (Louisville: Westminster John Knox, 2004), 127.
20 Andrew Riley goes so far as to argue that the primary function of hate here is metaphorical, connoting an abrogated covenant. Thus, he translates v. 28: "on account of his disloyalty to them (this is because he forsook his covenant with them)." Andrew Riley, *Divine and Human Hate in the Ancient Near East: A Lexical and Contextual Analysis* (Gorgias Press, 2017), 53–56. In so arguing, Riley is drawing on earlier work that emphasizes the covenantal background of Deuteronomy. In a seminal study on love in Deuteronomy, Moran argued that the definition of אהב in Deuteronomy is mechanistic and non-emotive, similar to the meaning of love language in ancient Near Eastern covenantal texts. In demanding that vassals love their sovereigns, ancient Near Eastern kings and Deuteronomy's God are demanding that their subjects fulfill their covenant obligations to obey their sovereign partners; William L. Moran, "The Ancient Near Eastern Background of the Love of God in Deuteronomy," *Catholic Biblical Quarterly* 25/1 (1963): 77–87. While the covenantal character of God's relationship with Israel in Deuteronomy is clear, Lapsley argues, convincingly, that Deuteronomic love retains an affective meaning connotation; Jacqueline Lapsley, "Feeling Our Way: Love for God in Deuteronomy," *Catholic Biblical Quarterly* 65/3 (2003): 350–69. See Deut 12:31; Jer 44:4. With this the case, one would assume that hate retains an affecting meaning as well.
21 A similar argument drives Israel's accusation of God in Deut 1:27. There, too, God is accused of acting as a typical hater who harms the vulnerable.
22 In Chapter 2, we explored how metonymic descriptions of anger in English reveal an underlying model of embodied anger. In Chapter 7, we will see that metonymic descriptions of ḥrh in biblical Hebrew function similarly. Despite the pervasiveness of metonymic descriptions of anger, metonymy is used neither in English nor in biblical Hebrew to describe *snʾ*. It *is* used, however, to describe the targets of God's *snʾ*.
23 Even though the מצבה may have been erected as part of the cult of Yahweh, Deuteronomy nonetheless condemns it as illegitimate, along with sacred pillars and altars. See Nelson, *Deuteronomy*, 216.
24 In cognitive linguistic terms, the source entity serves as a vehicle to direct attention to the target entity. In another example, the abominations that God hates, in Jer 44:4, refer to idolatrous sacrifices or the act of sacrificing them. As such, either the instrument (sacrifice) or the action (sacrificing) stands for its user/actor (worshiper).
25 Bernd Heine, "The Body in Language: Observations from Grammaticalization," in *The Body in Language: Comparative Studies of Linguistic Embodiment*, ed. Matthias Brenzinger and Iwona Kraska-Szlenk (Leiden: Brill, 2014), 17, 26. Across languages, the body can be extended "to express also concepts belonging to other domains of human experience" such as social relations and human activity (14).
26 Heine, "The Body in Language," 29.
27 More examples in which God is the subject of hate: Deut 1:27; 9:28; 12:31; Hos 9:15; Amos 5:21; 6:8; Isa 1:14; 61:8; Jer 12:8; Zech 8:17; Mal 1:3; 2:16; Pss 5:6; 11:5; Prov 6:16.
28 Gordon Paul Hugenberger, *Marriage as a Covenant: A Study of Biblical Law and Ethics Governing Marriage Developed from the Perspective of Malachi* (Leiden: Brill, 1993), 48.

29 See Deut 24:1–4.
30 Hugenberger, *Marriage as a Covenant*, 48.
31 While some scholars interpret the verse figuratively and others interpret it literally but narrowly, a third group of scholars argue that the verse is simply too corrupt to read plainly. For a summary of viewpoints, see Hugenberger, *Marriage as a Covenant*, 48–51.
32 Hugenberger, *Marriage as a Covenant*, 83.
33 For example, Isa 61:8; Zech 8:17. See also Prov 6:16–19.

6 Broad Biblical *Ḥrh*-Script

History of the Study of Biblical Anger

Prior to the twenty-first century, much research on anger in the Hebrew Bible was theologically oriented, aimed at reconciling God's anger with his righteousness. Even as a range of scholarly methods of interpretation emerged, attention remained focused on justifying God's wrath. Any forays that were taken into studying biblical anger as a broader concept tended to revolve around distinguishing people's "wicked wrath" from God's righteous anger.[1]

An exception is Bruce Baloian's 1992 work, *Anger in the Old Testament*, which seeks to ascertain "the theological concepts that comprise a coherent psychology of God [in the Hebrew Bible]" by deriving "a coherent psychology of human anger [in the Hebrew Bible]."[2] Despite his innovative approach, Baloian finds few similarities between human and divine anger. Instead, he judges human anger as petty, irrational, and sinful, in contrast to God's anger, which he judges as rational, just, and loving.[3]

As we discussed in Chapter 2, more critically oriented work on the biblical concept of anger began in earnest in the twenty-first century, around the time that the prototype approach to the study of emotions was gaining traction. At first, modern researchers focused, more broadly, on unpacking the conceptual category EMOTION. Toward this end, they asked groups of respondents to list, for example, members of the EMOTION category and rate degrees to which various terms are good or poor examples of it. Notably, researchers found that anger was consistently rated as one of the best or the best example of an emotion. It is not surprising, then, that anger was one of the first emotions—if not the first emotion—studied using the prototype approach. Biblical scholars took note and began to apply the approach to the study of biblical anger.

DOI: 10.4324/9781003348719-6

Broad Biblical Ḥrh-Script

Ellen van Wolde, one of the first scholars to apply the prototype approach to the Bible, observes that anger passages resemble one another, but do not share a consistent set of common traits.[4] In keeping with the classical view of conceptual categories, earlier research had aimed to identify anger's core traits. Yet, as van Wolde observes, when we scour the Bible in search of any defining traits, we find only typical traits. *Ḥrh* is usually ascribed to parties with power, status, and stature who are responding to disregard for their authority, but, periodically, it describes the response of a disempowered party. *Ḥrh* often precipitates a lethal response, but sometimes effects no response.

Drawing on George Lakoff and Zoltán Kövecses's work on modern English anger, van Wolde proposes a four-staged biblical anger-script: report of an offense or offending event; anger rises to the head; a loss of control ensues; which is followed by an act of retribution.[5] The script accurately characterizes many passages in the Bible, but it does not account for the diverse expressions of anger that are reflective of multiple overlapping narrower *ḥrh* scripts.

We refer to the widest range of traits that elicits the word *ḥrh* as the Broad Biblical *Ḥrh*-Script.[6] It is as follows:

Script	Conceptual Metaphor
1 Object disregards subject's authority	
2 Subject gets angry	Hot substance fills the body
3 Subject harms the object	

Subject, Object, and Antecedent of Ḥrh

Some biblical scholars identify the core cause of biblical anger to be "frustration." While this may be a trigger of anger, the term "frustration" itself is quite vague; it could imply sadness, shame, anger, or any combination of the three.[7] Matthew Schlimm and van Wolde suggest that anger results from a perceived wrongdoing. As van Wolde sees it, the biblical anger-script begins in the same way as the modern anger-script: in both scripts, anger is aroused in response to an appraisal of an offense. In fact, as we saw in Chapter 2, the idealized model of anger has embedded in it a triggering hindrance of power or disrespect, which presumes that the subject has power to confront the transgressor.[8]

Analogously, the idealized concept of *ḥrh*, as laid out in the Broad Biblical *Ḥrh*-Script, is a disregard for authority committed against

64 Broad Biblical Ḥrh-Script

parties with "power, status, and stature."[9] Most notably, God, who is *the* dominant party in the Bible, is also the most common subject of *ḥrh*. Moreover, descriptions of divine *ḥrh* are frequently paired with assertions of God's dominance—specifically, that he is king or the most powerful warrior.[10] Beyond this, twenty-one out of the twenty-six named individuals who get angry in the Bible are political leaders (kings, leaders, masters) or high-ranking family members. The dominant parties are angered by illicit relations and disobedience, likely because these behaviors threaten the security, wealth, or well-being of the family for which they are responsible. Similarly, political leaders are angered by rebellion and treachery that threaten the stability of the existing political structure.[11] Broadly put, the concept represented by the term *ḥrh* presumes a social standing of dominance.

While it may not be surprising that the Bible frequently ascribes *ḥrh* to disregarded authorities, it *is* surprising that the Bible virtually reserves *ḥrh* language for this single category of individual and type of wrongdoing. Throughout the Bible, *ḥrh* does not describe a wife's response to an oppressive husband; it does not describe the response of political subjects to wrongful treatment by their king; it does not describe the response of those who fall victim to mere accidents. This suggests that while a power dynamic of dominance is prototypical of both anger and *ḥrh*, it is more central to the *ḥrh* than it is to anger.

A "Container" of Ḥrh

Diverse cultures "seem to conceptualize human beings as containers, and anger or its counterpart as some kind of substance (a fluid or gas) inside the container."[12] This is not surprising. Since human beings share in common physical bodies, it is reasonable to expect that they share some similar conceptions about their experience of anger, regardless of where and when they live.

As we saw in Chapter 2, modern English anger is conceived as a hot liquid or gas that fills the body. The heat of anger rises in temperature, putting pressure on the container (the body) until it explodes out of the body. This is reflected, for example, in the phrases "He was filled with anger," "Don't get hot under the collar," "They were having a heated argument," and "You make my blood boil."[13]

As van Wolde already pointed out, biblical metaphors and metonymies of *ḥrh* indicate that *ḥrh* is conceived, similarly, as heat that is contained in the body and that rises to the head until it settles in the nose and the mouth.[14] The association of *ḥrh* with heat is evident, perhaps most obviously in the more concrete meaning of the lexeme itself. The root *ḥrh* means "to be angry" and "to be hot." Beyond this, the root *'ap* means both "anger" and "nose"; and the phrase *ḥrh 'ap*, which could literally be translated as "his nose became hot," in practice denotes "he became angry."[15] The centrality of heat to the biblical concept of *ḥrh* is apparent also in portrayals of God burning his objects of *ḥrh* with fire that shoots from his nose or mouth.[16]

Van Wolde proposes that the modern and biblical anger-scripts diverge at the point of anger's arousal, for the modern conception of anger anticipates an attempt at control and biblical anger does not. In a similar vein, Lakoff and Kövecses suggest that modern English anger is conceived as building up inside the body. The subject attempts to control it but fails. This is indicated in expressions such as, "He was bursting in anger," "She blew up at me," and "I won't tolerate your outbursts."

An uncontrolled response does not seem, however, to be particularly central to the idealized concept of biblical *ḥrh*. *Ḥrh* is associated, in generally equal measure, with destructive reprisal *and* tempered or even benign response.[17] In fact, in a number of instances, angered parties appear to exercise control over their *ḥrh* and even engage in planful processes of deliberation prior to reprisal.[18] On the flip side, some passages that do portray uncontrolled *ḥrh* incorporate special features that may signal their distinctiveness, such as attributing human *ḥrh* to the spirit of God.[19] We suggest that uncontrolled *ḥrh* is not central to the Broad Biblical *Ḥrh*-Script. It is central, rather, to a more narrowly applied narrative variant, specifically, the Outsider-Targeted *Ḥrh* Script.

Importantly, the Broad Biblical *Ḥrh*-Script does not define actual examples of *ḥrh*, nor is it the only *ḥrh*-script in the Bible. It represents the idealized sequence of traits that is anticipated when no context is provided. Actual examples of *ḥrh* may resemble the Broad Biblical *Ḥrh*-Script model but, since they are contextualized, they will also possess details that are not central to the wider model. These details may be central to a narrower set of contexts, such as when *ḥrh* targets kin or is borne by God. Alternatively, they may not be anticipated or central to *ḥrh*-script at all. Instead, they may be specific to a particular instance of *ḥrh*. In light of these diverse possibilities, identifying the idealized model of *ḥrh*, as represented by the Broad Biblical *Ḥrh*-Script, allows us to better understand the distinctive tenor and connotation of *ḥrh* in specific passages.

Notes

1 For a brief summary, see Deena Grant, *Divine Anger in the Hebrew Bible* (Washington, D.C.: CBA, 2014): 418–24.
2 Bruce Edward Baloian, *Anger in the Old Testament* (New York: Peter Lang, 1992), 4.
3 Baloian, *Anger in the Old Testament*, 4.
4 Selected twenty-first-century works on biblical anger include: Matthew Michael, "Anger Management and Biblical Characters: A Study of 'Angry

Exchange' among Characters of Hebrew Narrative," *Old Testament Abstracts* 28/2 (2015): 451–80. Grant, *Divine Anger in the Hebrew Bible*; Matthew Schlimm, *From Fratricide to Forgiveness* (Winona Lake: Eisenbrauns, 2011); Ellen van Wolde, *Reframing Biblical Studies: When Language and Text Meet Culture, Cognition, and Context* (Winona Lake: Eisenbrauns, 2009), 60–71; Paul A. Kruger, "A Cognitive Interpretation of the Emotion of Anger in the Hebrew Bible," *Journal of North-West Semitic Languages* 26/1 (2000): 181–93.

5 Van Wolde, *Reframing Biblical Studies*, 62, 73.
6 Previous scholars who worked on biblical anger did not limit their discussion to a single term (for an exception, see Samantha Joo, *Provocation and Punishment: The Anger of God in the Book of Jeremiah and Deuteronomistic Theology* (Berlin: De Gruyter, 2006). Since we, however, are studying emotion concepts as they are represented in language, and we want to ensure that we are identifying traits central to a single concept, we generally restrict our examination of passages to those that cite *ḥrh*. Therefore, in Chapters 6 and 7, we refer to the concept under study as *ḥrh*, except when we are addressing the work of others; there, we refer to it as anger. We break this pattern in Chapter 8, which discusses anger in Old Poetic and prophetic texts, because *ḥrh* is not the preferred term to designate a response to disregarded authority that precipitates harm. For more on this, see Chapter 8.
7 Schlimm, *From Fratricide to Forgiveness*, 57.
8 Fitness, "Anger in the Workplace," 147–62; Shaver et al., "Emotion Knowledge," 1074, 1077.
9 Schlimm, *From Fratricide to Forgiveness*, 57; van Wolde, *Reframing Biblical Studies*, 60–64.
10 See Exod 15:7, 17; Jer 10:10, 24–25; Ezek 20:8, 33–37; Zeph 3:8–9; Ps 2:5–6.
11 See Gen 39:19; Exod 11:8; 1 Sam 20:30; 2 Sam 13:21; Esth 1:12; Dan 3:13. Van Wolde describes anger as "embedded in a hierarchical framework," pointing out that it is predominantly ascribed to male protagonists who are socially higher than their object of anger; *Reframing Biblical Studies*, 72. Schlimm notes that this is not always the case, pointing to a small number of instances of anger between equals, or where the power dynamics are unclear; Schlimm, *Fratricide to Forgiveness*, 57. I would add that even those times when anger *is* ascribed to the less dominant party, the text avoids explicitly describing it as such. For example, 1 Sam 20:34 awkwardly avoids stating that Jonathan is angry *at* Saul and instead describes him as walking away in anger. Similarly, 2 Sam 6:8 avoids stating that David is angry *at* God. See also 1 Sam 1:6; Esth 1:18; 2:21.
12 Kövecses recognizes that there are cultural differences even within this model. For example, as van Wolde remarks, as well, both biblical Hebrew and Japanese conceive of the body as a container of anger, but they differ with regard to anger's precise location and trajectory. In Japanese, the locus of anger seems to be the belly or chest, from which it rises to the head if not controlled. Zoltán Kövecses, "The Concept of Anger: Universal or Culture Specific," *Psychopathology* 33/4 (2000): 159–70; van Wolde, *Reframing Biblical Studies*, 64.
13 Lakoff, *Women, Fire, and Dangerous Things*, 381–83; Kövecses, *Metaphors of Anger, Pride, and Love*, 11–14.
14 Van Wolde, *Reframing Biblical Studies*, 63, 72; Kruger, "A Cognitive Interpretation of the Emotion of Anger in the Hebrew Bible."
15 Grant, *Divine Anger in the Hebrew Bible*, 22–27. Counting its attestations both with and without חרה, אף is the most common anger root in the Hebrew

Bible, describing human anger 40 times and divine anger 170 times. Cognates include Arabic *ḥarra* and Aramaic *ḥrr* of the Targumim, which both mean "burn" (or the latter, "be blackened"). Botterweck et al., "חרה *ḥārâ*."
16 For example, Isa 30:27; Ezek 38:18; Jer 22:12.
17 Kruger recognizes that biblical anger has a wide range of responses which can be verbal and physical and can connote uneasiness and withdrawal. Kruger, "A Cognitive Interpretation of Anger in the Hebrew Bible," 182.
18 For example, when angered, Ahasuerus leaves the room, perhaps to deliberate and cool off (Esth 7:7). Even Dinah's brothers do not actually act uncontrollably. Instead, they pursue a deliberate plan for recompense (Genesis 34).
19 For example, Saul's anger at the Ammonites (1 Sam 11:6) and Samson's anger at the Ashkelonites (Judg 14:19). These both be interpreted as examples of uncontrolled anger, and they are also both associated with the uncommon phenomenon of God's spirit falling upon the angry parties.

7 Narrative *Ḥrh*-Scripts

Outsider-Targeted *Ḥrh*-Script

- Target disregards the subject's authority.
- *Ḥrh* burns within the subject.
- Subject murders the target and others.
- Threat is annulled.

Kin-Targeted *Ḥrh*-Script

- Target disregards subject's authority.
- *Ḥrh* burns within subject.
- No punishment or tempered punishment for the target.
- Threat persists.

We find two prominent variants of the Broad Biblical *Ḥrh*-Script in biblical narratives: the Outsider-Targeted *Ḥrh*-Script and the Kin-Targeted *Ḥrh*-Script. These narrative variants align with the broader conceptual model in featuring a disregard for authority and an ensuing arousal of *ḥrh* as heat that fills the body. They also incorporate an additional trait that is not central to the Broad Biblical *Ḥrh*-Script: an outcome. As with *sn'*, the anticipated course of *ḥrh* in biblical narratives hinges on the relationship between the subject and target. However, whereas the course of hate pivots on gender, the course of *ḥrh* pivots on kinship.

The theme of disregarded authority is central to the Outsider-Targeted *Ḥrh*-Script. *Ḥrh* at outsiders—by whom we mean those who are identified neither as family members nor as members of an ethno-community—is typically elicited by violations against political or familial domains of authority and precipitates a lethal response. Passages that describe such *ḥrh* tend to focus on the provoker's outsider status, in order to justify lethal *ḥrh*; since outsiders do not necessarily respect the locally mandated authority, angered parties must respond lethally in order to reassert their authority over their compromised domains and discourage future disregard.

DOI: 10.4324/9781003348719-7

Authority is also central to the Kin-Targeted Ḥrh-Script, though not in the same way. Ḥrh at kin is almost always nonlethal and is often completely benign. In fact, offenses that elicit lethal ḥrh when committed by an outsider, such as illicit relations and political treachery, typically elicit no consequence when committed by a family member.

In biblical narratives, the arousal of ḥrh at kin also foreshadows a coming loss of authority. There are two reasons for this. First, disregarded authority is a sign that the family hierarchy is eroding from within. Beyond this, self-interest to protect the family, coupled with affection that typically characterizes the kinship bond, may diminish the force of ḥrh, rendering the angered kin unprepared to act harshly enough to restore authority.

Identifying the Broad Biblical Ḥrh-Script helps us recognize the distinct nuances embedded in the notion of ḥrh within the narrower scope of these variant scripts. In this same vein, identifying the narrative ḥrh-scripts helps us recognize and appreciate the ways that specific passages elaborate on and modify them in order to convey distinct messages.[1]

Outsider-Targeted Ḥrh-Script

Genesis 34

Ḥrh at outsiders is typically unforgiving. Even so, a distinct nuance of Genesis 34 lies in the angered brothers' unduly harsh reprisal:

- Shechem has relations with Dinah.
- Dinah's brothers are distressed and very angry.
- Dinah's brothers refuse an offer to reconcile.
- Dinah's brothers murder Shechem and plunder his community.

Jacob's sons become angry when Shechem has relations with their sister, Dinah (34:2). Scholars have long debated whether these relations constitute rape or seduction.[2] Either way, in the ancient world, "all sex between a man and the female ward of non-consenting male guardians, generally a father and/or brothers, is rape" that is "akin to theft of property."[3] In this light, Shechem's *theft* of Dinah's chastity is an infringement on Jacob's familial domain that is both irretrievable and humiliating to his family.

Jacob does not respond, which leads Dinah's brothers to do so instead.[4] The narrative describes the brothers as distressed and angry, after which they pursue lethal reprisal. The narrative also states that the brothers' ḥrh stems from the fact that Shechem's offense is an "outrage in Israel" (34:7).[5]

ובני יעקב באו מן-השדה כשמעם ויתעצבו האנשים ויחר להם מאד כי-נבלה עשה בישראל
לשכב את-בת-יעקב וכן לא יעשה

The rare phrase "outrage in Israel" is used also in Joshua 7 to describe a theft that elicits God's ḥrh (וכי-עשה נבלה בישראל, 7:15).[6] In both Genesis 34 and Joshua 7, provokers take what does not belong to them: Shechem takes Dinah, and Achan steals God's devoted objects. In both passages, as well, angered parties execute wide-scale and lethal reprisal. Dinah's angered brothers kill Shechem, his father, and plunder his entire town. The angered deity allows thirty-six Hebrew men to die in battle and demands that Achan be executed along with his family (Gen 34:25–29; Josh 7:5–11).

The aim of ḥrh in Genesis 34 and Joshua 7 appears analogous as well: to dissuade future disregard for a domain of authority by broadcasting the consequences of violating it. In Joshua 7, God's ḥrh turns away only after Joshua erects a public monument to memorialize the events that surround it (וישב יהוה מחרון אפו, 7:24–26). In Genesis 34, the brothers unabashedly respond to their father, who critiques their angry reprisal, with a question that presumes a wider audience: "Should our sister be treated like a whore?" (הכזונה יעשה את-אחותינו, 34:31).[7]

Schlimm suggests that Hamor's generous offer, that the tribes resolve the conflict through intermarriage (34:9), does not appease the brothers because Dinah's rape is one of "anger's worst problems" that demands extreme reprisal.[8] This is unlikely. Rape occurs elsewhere in the Bible, and even incites ḥrh elsewhere, without precipitating a massacre.[9] More likely, the brothers pursue lethal reprisal partly to broadcast what happens to outsiders when they violate the family of Jacob. Indeed, the passage stresses Shechem's status as a foreigner, describing him as a Hivite at the outset of the narrative—and later, judging the Hivites as unmarriageable because, unlike the family of Jacob, they are uncircumcised (34:2, 14–15). The public aim of ḥrh is signaled also by the brothers' defense of their actions, which, as we just mentioned, presumes a wider audience (34:31).

The existence of another idealized model of ḥrh (represented by the Kin-Targeted Ḥrh-Script) may account for why Hamor proposes that the two groups become "one nation" (והיינו לעם אחד, 34:16). Hamor is suggesting "something akin to an inter-clan covenant which would create an affinity between the two non-kinship groups."[10] He may presume that, as is anticipated in cases of kin-targeted ḥrh, when the two communities are tied as kin, the consequences of the brothers' ḥrh will be tempered.[11] In this light, Hamor's proposal stands as a reminder that while lethal reprisal may be typical, it is not the brothers' only recourse.

The brothers refuse. In fact, Hamor's offer that the entire town marry into Jacob's family foreshadows the greater scope of the brothers' reprisal, which is directed at the entire town. The brothers' negative response stands contrary to God's allowance, in Joshua 7, that Israel they may avert his lethal *ḥrh* by returning the stolen objects.[12]

Genesis 39

Genesis 39 offers an unusual example of *ḥrh* at a *favored* outsider.

- Potiphar raises Joseph to chief of household.
- Joseph (allegedly) violates Potiphar's wife.
- Potiphar becomes angry.
- Potiphar sends Joseph to the king's prison.

Soon after Potiphar promotes Joseph to manage his entire estate (39:4–6), Potiphar's wife accuses Joseph of trying to violate her (39:17–18). In her accusation, she refers to Joseph as "the Hebrew slave whom you brought into our house" (העבד העברי אשר-הבאת לנו לצחק בי, 39:17). By describing Joseph in this way, Potiphar's wife reminds her husband that he foolishly brought this disregard upon himself. Her reminder may even be an implicit critique of Potiphar's ability to defend his familial domain of authority.[13]

Potiphar's wife stresses also that Joseph is a foreigner, twice referring to him as a Hebrew (39:14, 17). With this, she may be attempting to elicit from her husband lethal *ḥrh*, such as is anticipated toward an outsider. Potiphar does get angry but does not demand Joseph's execution. Instead, he condemns Joseph to the king's prison (39:19b–20). Gordon Wenham remarks that this "is a somewhat unexpected punishment" since, in Deuteronomy and elsewhere, convicted rapists are executed.[14] Wenham suggests that Joseph's protestations of innocence convince Potiphar that his wife might be fabricating the story. But Wenham concedes that nowhere does the text hint that Potiphar doubts his wife.[15]

Joseph's confinement to the king's prison is a public assertion of Potiphar's high authority—those who disregard Potiphar are imprisoned by the king. It also conveys Joseph's intermediate status; Joseph is a target of *ḥrh* who is favored but not kin (וימצא יוסף חן בעיניו, 39:4). Potiphar's punishment is, correspondingly, punitive but not immediately lethal. He does not condemn Joseph to death but also does not shield him from execution; inmates in the king's prison are sometimes, but not always, executed.[16]

Potiphar's temperance may also underscore God's intervention. God grants Joseph the success that affords him his unusual status as a favored outsider, and it is this status that protects him from Potiphar's immediately lethal *ḥrh* (וירא אדניו כי יהוה אתו וכל אשר-הוא עשה מצליח בידו, 39:3).

Esther 3 and Daniel 3

The account of Haman's *ḥmh* at Mordechai, in Esther 3, and Nebuchadnezzar's *ḥmh* at the three Jews in Daniel 3 underscores the precarious state of the Jewish "outsider" in diaspora.[17]

Esther 3

- Mordechai is raised to high authority.
- Mordechai refuses to bow to Haman.
- Haman gets angry.
- Haman seeks to execute Mordechai and his entire people.

Daniel 3

- Nebuchadnezzar appoints three Jews over the affairs of Babylon.
- Three Jews refuse to bow to Nebuchadnezzar's statue.
- Nebuchadnezzar gets angry.
- Three Jews refuse to bow.
- Nebuchadnezzar throws them into a fire.

Mordechai elicits Haman's lethal *ḥmh* when he refuses to bow to him, thus disregarding Haman's newly ascendant status (3:1–6):

אחר הדברים האלה גדל המלך אחשורוש את-המן בן-המדתא האגגי וינשאהו וישם את-כסאו מעל כל-השרים אשר אתו: וכל-עבדי המלך אשר-בשער המלך כרעים ומשתחוים להמן כי-כן צוה-לו המלך ומרדכי לא יכרע ולא ישתחוה.וירא המן כי-אין מרדכי כרע ומשתחוה לו וימלא המן חמה: ויבז בעיניו לשלח יד במרדכי לבדו כי-הגידו לו את-עם מרדכי ויבקש המן להשמיד את-כל-היהודים אשר בכל-מלכות אחשורוש עם מרדכי ויאמר המן למלך ישנו עם-אחד מפזר ומפרד בין העמים בכל מדינות מלכותך ודתיהם שנות מכל-עם ואת-דתי המלך אינם עשים למלך אין-שוה להניחם

Adele Berlin suggests that the identification of Mordechai as Jewish shows that it is his Jewishness that compels him to refuse to bow (3:4).[18] Indeed, Haman warns the king that the Jews' "separateness"—in particular, their singular observance of a distinct set of laws—compels them to disregard the king's law (3:7). Haman also reminds Ahasuerus that the Jews are scattered across all the provinces of the land. This may be an implicit warning that one Jew's disregard for the authority of the king's adviser here could trigger a wider disregard for the king's own authority across the land.

Mordechai's identity as Jewish also accounts for the broad scope of Haman's *ḥmh*. Though Haman becomes angry when Mordechai offends him, his *ḥmh* turns lethal only when he hears that Mordechai is Jewish. It is at this point that Haman seeks to kill the entire Jewish people (3:5–6). With the king's consent, Haman publicizes the lethal decree, sending copies far and wide, across the king's provinces, in the many different scripts and languages and to be displayed publicly (3:12–15):

ויקראו ספרי המלך בחדש הראשון בשלושה עשר יום בו ויכתב ככל-אשר-צוה המן אל
אחשדרפני-המלך ואל-פחות אשר על-מדינה ומדינה ואל-שרי עם ועם מדינה ומדינה
ככתבה ועם ועם כלשונו בשם המלך אחשורש נכתב ונחתם בטבעת המלך: ונשלוח ספרים
ביד הרצים את-כל-היהודים מנער ועד-זקן טף ונשים ביום אחד בשלושה עשר לחדש
שנים-עשר הוא-חדש אדר ושללם לבוז: פתשגן הכתב להנתן דת בכל-מדינה ומדינה גלוי
לכל-העמים להיות עתדים ליום הזה

In this way, Haman publicly broadcasts the harsh consequences of provoking his *ḥmh* by disregarding his newly ascendant status.[19]

Daniel 3 offers another example of *ḥmh* over a refusal to bow; Nebuchadnezzar gets angry when he hears that Shedrach, Meshach, and Abednego have defied his order to bow to his statue.[20] As Haman stressed to Ahasuerus, these informants stress that the men's foreign identity, as Jews, is what compels them to disobey the king (3:12):

איתי גברין יהודאין די-מנית יתהון על-עבידת מדינת בבל שדרך מישך ועבד נגו גבריא
אלך לא-שמו עליך מלכא טעם לאלהיך לא פלחין ולצלם דהבא די הקימת
לא סגדין:

They describe the Jews as separate from the rest of the king's subjects, following their own laws and refusing to worship the king's gods. They also remind the king that he himself placed them as heads over the affairs of the province of Babylon. This reminder may also be a warning that the king failed to defend his own authority, similar to the warning that Potiphar received from his wife.

Nebuchadnezzar does not execute the Jews, as would be anticipated by the Outsider-Targeted *Ḥrh*-Script. Instead, he advises them to reform their ways. The uncharacteristic temperance of *ḥmh* is conveyed by the addition of the rarer root *rgz*, which has a less intense connotation—similar, perhaps, to the English word "annoy" (באדין נבוכדנצר ברגז וחמה, 3:13).[21]

Nebuchadnezzar may think that his authority is better served, at this point, by keeping the Jews alive, so that they publicly reject their God

74 *Narrative Ḥrh-Scripts*

in favor of fealty to the king. It is toward this end that Nebuchadnezzar asks them, "Could any god rescue you from the furnace?" (3:15). Unfortunately, for the king, the Jews do not have a change of heart. Instead, they proclaim that they need not adhere to the king's orders because their God will rescue them (3:16–18). When the Jews reaffirm their rejection of the king's authority, he becomes lethally angry. The growing intensity of Nebuchadnezzar's *ḥmh* is communicated in several ways (3:19):

באדין נבוכדנצר התמלי חמא וצלם אנפוהי אשתנו על-שדרך מישך ועבד נגו ענה ואמר
למזא לאתונא חד-שבעה על די חזא למזיא

The moderating root *rgz* is dropped from the description of this second bout of *ḥmh*, and the king loses control over his own visage. The king then acts senselessly, demanding that the furnace be raised to seven times its usual heat, even though, presumably, the furnace's regular temperature is already lethal.

Van Wolde posits that a loss of control, such as Nebuchadnezzar exhibits here, is a typical feature. We argue that a loss of control is central, specifically, to the outsider-targeted *ḥrh*. It is displayed here via a distorted face and irrational behavior, and serves to strengthen this polemical rendering of a Babylonian king being bested by the Jewish deity. Indeed, the king's act of *ḥmh* proves futile in the face of God's redemption, and, in fact, the king ends up blessing the very deity whose authority threatens his own (אלההון די-שדרך מישך ועבד נגו בריך, 3:28).

Kin-Targeted *Ḥrh*-Script[22]

1 Samuel 20

1 Samuel 20 emphasizes the impotence of *ḥrh* when it is directed at kin.

- Jonathan deceived Saul.
- Saul gets angry at Jonathan.
- Saul throws a spear.
- Jonathan disobeys Saul.

Saul becomes angry at his son Jonathan when he aids a pretender to Saul's throne (ויחר אף שאול ביהונתן, 20:30–33). In contrast to the lethal *ḥrh* triggered in other instances of treachery and disobedience (e.g., 1 Samuel 18; Daniel 3), Saul does not kill Jonathan. Instead, he demands that his son reaffirm his loyalty and annul the threat to Saul's rule by delivering David into his hands (20:30–33).

When Jonathan protests, Saul throws a spear in his direction (ויטל שאול את החנית להכתו, 20:33). David Tsumura and Ralph Klein interpret Saul's action as an attempt to kill Jonathan.[23] This is unlikely. The infinitive construct verb form להכתו, which describes Saul's assault, does not necessarily signify a lethal strike.[24] Moreover, Saul's spear appears to miss Jonathan, even though the father and son are close enough to be in conversation. Furthermore, after Saul throws the spear, Jonathan realizes that the king is determined to kill *David*, not him (20:33). It seems more likely, then, that Saul throws his spear in an act of frustration or as a benign message, rather than as an attempt to kill his own son. This would explain why Jonathan does not run away in fear and why Saul makes no move to pursue him when he leaves.

A nonlethal response is rational within a kinship context. Were Saul to kill his son and heir, he would compromise the perpetuation of his own dynasty. Saul says as much when he warns Jonathan that his son will not be king as long as he supports David (20:31). After warning Jonathan that his behavior threatens his own chance at becoming king, Saul would not try to compromise it himself by killing Jonathan.[25]

When viewed against the larger backdrop of 1 and 2 Samuel, Saul's relatively benign *ḥrh* may be attributed to his affection for his son. In his song of eulogy for Saul and Jonathan, David declares that the father and son loved each other in life and remain bonded in death (שאול ויהונתן הנאהבים והנעימם, 2 Sam 1:23). Even if this poem were unknown to the author of 1 Samuel 20, it brings to the fore the theme of paternal attachment, which may inform the representation of Saul's *ḥrh* in 1 Samuel 20.[26]

Ultimately, this kin-targeted *ḥrh* is ineffective in countering the disregard for authority and even foreshadows a greater loss of authority. The next morning, Jonathan disobeys his father's command and proceeds to help David (20:35–42). God has already ordained the end of Saul's dynasty (1 Sam 15:28). The king's impotent *ḥrh* in response to his son's disregard is a sign that the end is near.[27]

Esther 1

Ahasuerus becomes angry at his wife, Vashti, when she disobeys his command to exhibit herself publicly (ויקצף המלך מאד וחמתו בערה בו, 1:12). On the advice of his adviser, who warns that Vashti's intransigent behavior could foster a culture of rebellion among wives across the kingdom (1:16–22), he then banishes her. Thereafter, Ahasuerus's *ḥmh* subsides (2:1).

- Vashti refuses to exhibit herself.
- Ahasuerus gets angry at Vashti.

76 *Narrative Ḥrh-Scripts*

- Ahasuerus exiles Vashti.
- Ahasuerus's *ḥrh* subsides.

The course of *ḥmh* anticipated by variant Kin-Targeted *Ḥrh*-Script may explain the speed and eagerness with which the king's advisers seek to replace Vashti (2:2–4). They may be concerned that, over time, when the king's *ḥmh* dissipates, he will contravene his own decree to take his wife back. In fact, the passage implies as much (2:1). Indeed, when the king's *ḥmh* subsides, he uses the passive construction to refer to his action against Vashti, stating "that which was decreed against her." In this way, he distances himself from his own angry reprisal.

אחר הדברים האלך כשך חמת המלך אחשורוש זכר את-ושתי ואת אשר-עשתה ואת אשר-נגזר עליה

The wives' rebellion, which Ahasuerus's advisers warn about, does not come to pass. But the king's waning *ḥmh* does foreshadow his weakening authority as reflected in two other egregious offenses against his rule: Bigthan and Teresh plot to assassinate him; and Haman plots to kill his wife and her people (2:21; 3:6). In both cases, the king is ill-prepared to counter the threat, so someone else does it for him.

Genesis 30

Jacob's *ḥrh* at Rachel, in Genesis 30, is tempered by love.

- Rachel accuses Jacob of withholding a child.
- Jacob gets angry at Rachel.
- Jacob remedies Rachel's problem.

In Genesis 30, Jacob gets angry at Rachel when she pleads with him to heal her barrenness (ויחר אף יעקב ברחל, 30:2). At first glance, Jacob's *ḥrh* seems odd because Rachel does not commit a clear offense. In directing her plea to him, however, Rachel is implying that Jacob has the power to grant her children but refuses to do so. Moreover, by warning Jacob that she will die lest he grant her children, Rachel is threatening to revoke his status as her husband if he shirks this spousal obligation (30:1).

The absence of punitive *ḥrh* is not surprising, since Rachel's affront is relatively minor. It is notable, however, that Jacob sets aside his *ḥrh* entirely and pursues a plan to alleviate his wife's suffering. The earlier reference to Jacob's love for Rachel (ויאהב יעקב את-רחל, 29:18) hints that his affection for her is what effectively renders his *ḥrh* benign.[28]

Genesis 4

Genesis 4 offers an exceptionally deviant case of *ḥrh*, as it represents a large departure from the course of *ḥrh* anticipated by the Kin-Targeted *Ḥrh*-Script.

- God prefers Abel's sacrifice.
- Cain becomes angry and sad.
- Cain kills Abel.
- Cain is punished.

When God prefers Abel's offering, Cain gets angry at Abel and kills him (4:5–11):

ואל-קין ואל-מנחתו לא שעה ויחר לקין מאד ויפלו פניו: ויאמר יהוה אל-קין למה חרה לך
ולמה נפלו פניך: הלוא אם-תיטיב שאת ואם לא תיטיב לפתח רבץ ואליך תשוקתו ואתה
תמשל-בו: ויאמר קין אל-הבל אחיו ויהי בהיותם בשדה ויקם קין אל-הבל אחיו ויהרגהו:
ויאמר יהוה אל-קין אי הבל אחיך ויאמר לא ידעתי השמר אחי אנכי: ויאמר מה עשית קול
דמי אחיך צעקים אלי מן-האדמה: ועתה ארור מן-האדמה אשר פצתה את-פיה לקחת את-
דמי אחיך מידך

Scholars have long speculated about why God prefers Abel's offering over Cain's.[29] Westermann argues, however, that the passage is simply not interested in explaining *why* God prefers it. Indeed, in its present form, the text focuses on Cain's response to God's rejection.[30]

The exceptional nature of Cain's *ḥrh* is conveyed by the narrator's emphasis on Abel's identity as his brother. The narrator repeats this point four times within the span of four verses, as if to say that lethal *ḥrh* at kin cannot be believed (4:8, 9, 10, 11).

Cain' *ḥrh* is denoted by the expression חרה לו, which literally means "it burns him." Mayer Gruber suggests that this syntax, in contrast to the more common phrase חרה אף, emphasizes Cain's internal experience of *ḥrh*, which encompasses both sadness or depression. As evidence, Gruber points out that Cain's face falls (4:5), and a fallen face was widely regarded as a symptom of sadness in the ancient Near East.[31] For Gruber, the passage likely describes a case of "depressive sadness."

Gruber is correct to underline Cain's sadness, though not to the exclusion of *ḥrh*.[32] It has been proposed that the coupling of *ḥrh* and sadness connotes depression and is experienced by Cain as alienation. Regardless, Cain responds with unexpectedly lethal *ḥrh*. It is this isolating sad-*ḥrh* that compels him to kill Abel, thus protesting a role that should be natural: that of his brother's keeper (4:9).

Cain's distinctive *ḥrh* foreshadows a loss greater than what provokes his *ḥrh*. Cain competes with his brother for the favor of their divine patriarch. But when Cain's sad-ḥrh compels him to remove the competition, he does not attain a closer relationship with the deity. On the contrary, God banishes Cain from his presence (4:13–14).

Notes

1. Further examples of outsider-targeted anger can be found in Genesis 27, Judges 14–15, 1 Samuel 17, 2 Samuel 13, Esther 7, and Judges 14–15. It is possible that the degree of kinship accounts, even more narrowly, for differences among examples of anger at kin, but it is hard to know for certain.
2. Much of the debate hinges on the definition of ויענה (34:2) which may or may not be translated as "he seized her."
3. Propp, "Kinship in 2 Samuel 13," *Catholic Biblical Quarterly* 55 (1993): 41.
4. On the violation that is rape, see Deut 22:28. Jacob, the elder father, is clearly marginalized. He no longer shepherds in the field (34:5) and Hamor directs his conciliatory proposal to the other "men" of the family, not him. See Ingo Kottsieper, "We Have a Little Sister," in *Families and Family Relations as Represented in Early Judaisms and Early Christianities: Texts and Fictions*, ed. Athalya Brenner and Jan Willem van Henten (Leiderdorp: Deo, 2000), 49–80; Ronald T. Hyman, "Final Judgment: The Ambiguous Moral Question that Culminates Genesis 34," *Jewish Biblical Quarterly* 28 (2000): 93–101.
5. It is not exactly the rape but, more specifically, the fact that the rape is an "outrage." The brothers are saddened when they hear about the offense, but they are very angry because it was an outrage in Israel (34:7). Kruger suggests that sadness arises when the angered party believes that the thwarted goal, such as Dinah's virginity, can no longer be reinstated; Kruger, "A Cognitive Interpretation of the Emotion of Anger in the Hebrew Bible," *Journal of North-west Semitic Languages* 27 (2001): 182. For a similar example, see Gen 4:1–16.
6. For another example of an "outrage in Israel" triggering lethal anger, see 2 Sam 13:12.
7. Wyatt suggests that the brothers refer to Dinah not by name but only as "our sister" because they view Dinah as an element of property and her feelings are of no concern to them. Nicholas Wyatt, "The Story of Dinah and Shechem," *UF* 22 (1990): 433–58. Alternatively, they identify the victim only as their sister as a warning to those who violate the family of Jacob.
8. Schlimm, *From Fratricide to Forgiveness: The Language and Ethics of Anger in Genesis* (University Park: Penn State University Press, 2011), 161. He observes that in other cases of anger in Genesis, generosity *does* assuage anger's worst effects. Yet the examples that Schlimm offers of generosity appeasing anger elsewhere in Genesis (chapters 3 and 26) do not cite an anger term, so it is hard to know.
9. For example, 2 Samuel 13.
10. The passage may derive from a single narrative, but it may otherwise reflect an oral or a written tradition that was later reworked or combined with another. As one possibility, Rofé sees two versions in this account: an earlier version that was a saga about Israel's clan heroes; and the present form that is a polemic against intermarriage with impure gentiles; see Alexander Rofé, "Defilement of Virgins in Biblical Law and the Case of Dinah (Genesis 34)," *Bib* 86 (2005): 369–75. Westermann suggests, somewhat similarly, that a political account (Hamor source) was reworked into or combined with a source concerned with family matters—specifically, a violation of Jacob's family (Shechem source). Claus Westermann, *Genesis 12–36: A Continental*

Commentary, trans. John Scullion (Minneapolis: Augsburg Fortress, 1985), 536–39. Viewed in this light, Hamor's suggestion that the two groups intermarry may simply be "a matter of increasing the extent and wealth of a city by absorbing into it a nomadic group with large flocks," wholly unrelated to any sexual violation. While Westermann may be correct that economics was Hamor's main interest in an earlier iteration of the account, the current literary setting makes no mention of economics. For more on how marriage brings kin-like economic and social benefits, see Allen Guenther, "A Typology of Israelite Marriage: Kinship, Socioeconomic and Religious Factors," *Journal for the Study of Old Testament* 29 (2005): 387–407.

11 Westermann, *Genesis 12–36*, 536–39.
12 Another signal that the brothers' anger is exceptionally harsh lies in the word "very much /intense" (מאד, 34:7), a sentiment also reflected in Gen 49:5–7's reminiscence of this event.
13 Wenham suggests that by using שרת, which "always implies personal service," instead of the more common עבד, which can indicate menial jobs done by slaves, the passage highlights Joseph's rise in Potiphar's esteem; see Gordon Wenham, *Genesis 16–50* (Nashville: Thomas Nelson, 1994), 376.
14 See Deut 22:33–27.
15 Wenham, *Genesis 16–50*, 377.
16 The bread-maker is executed, while the cupbearer is set free (Gen 40:20–23).
17 *Ḥrh* is by far the most common word used to describe an urge to harm that is precipitated by disregarded authority. Nonetheless, a number of roots, such as *ḥmh*, which scholars typically translate as anger (or as a synonym thereof) do so as well. Consequently, we sometimes include the terms in our study. Nonetheless, since they carry similar connotations and since *ḥrh* is used to an overwhelmingly degree, we use the term *ḥrh* to refer to these scripts. On the nuances of various anger terms, see Grant, *Divine Anger in the Hebrew Bible*, 22–39.
18 Adele Berlin, *Esther: The Traditional Hebrew Text with the New JPS Translation* (Philadelphia: Jewish Publication Society, 2001), 37.
19 For another example, see 7:7–8. In this case, Ahasuerus's *ḥmh* turns lethal specifically when he perceives Haman advancing upon his wife (3:1) and interprets it as an act of political rebellion.
20 On the purpose of Nebuchadnezzar's statue, see John Goldingay, *Daniel* (Dallas: Word Books, 1989), 72–73; see also John Joseph Collins, Frank M. Cross, and Adela Yarbro Collins, *Daniel: A Commentary on the Book of Daniel* (Minneapolis: Augsburg Fortress, 1993), 186.
21 G. Vanoni, "רגז, *rāgaz*," *TDOT* 14:304–8.
22 For more examples of this script, beyond what is listed here, see Genesis 27:44 (the anger term used here is *ḥmh*) and 2 Samuel 13:21.
23 Tsumura translates v. 33 as "and then Saul tries to kill Jonathan"; see David T. Tsumura, *The First Book of Samuel* (Grand Rapids, Mich.: Eerdmans, 2007), 521; Ralph Klein, *1 Samuel* (Nashville: Thomas Nelson, 1983), 208. Though their translation is in line with the Septuagint and Dead Sea Scrolls, it is unlikely due to the reasons cited above.
24 See also Deut 25:3; 1 Kgs 20:35.
25 For an alternative interpretation, see P. Kyle McCarter, *II Samuel: A New Translation with Introduction, Notes, and Commentary* (Garden City: Doubleday, 1984), 339.
26 Notably, Jonathan grows angry shortly thereafter (ויקם יהונתן מן השלחן בחרי אף, 20:34). Jonathan's anger is one of the few examples of anger arising over the actions of an authority figure. Significantly, the text carefully refrains from stating that Jonathan is angry *at* Saul, casting him instead as angry at the situation.

80 *Narrative Ḥrh-Scripts*

27 Gen 31:35 offers another example of benign paternal anger.
28 In another example of benign *ḥrh*, David gets angry at Amnon for raping Tamar but he does not punish him. The Septuagint and Septuagint and 4QSam[a] explain that David responds benignly on account of his love for his son. David's response is especially notably juxtaposed against Absalom who respond to the rape with lethal hate.
29 Most suggestions focus on the quality of Cain's sacrifice versus the quality of Abel's sacrifice; see Judah Goldin, "The Youngest Son or Where Does Genesis 38 Belong?" *Journal of Biblical Literature* 96 (1977): 27–44; Bruce Waltke, "Cain and His Offering," *Westminster Theological Journal* 48/2 (1986): 212–30. Some suggest that the awkward transition between God's choice of Abel's sacrifice and Cain's murder of Abel (4:4–8) hints that in an earlier version of the account, a different event triggered the murder.
30 Westermann suggests that the portrait of Cain in Genesis 4 demonstrates that human "envy" is the most powerful trigger of conflict in humanity's history. Claus Westermann, *Genesis 1–11: A Continental Commentary* (Minneapolis: Fortress, 1990), 294. The passage does not cite, though, the biblical Hebrew term that is closest to English "envy": קנא.
31 Mayer Gruber, "The Tragedy of Cain and Abel: A Case of Depression," *Jewish Quarterly Review* 69 (1978): 91, 94. Kruger suggests that Cain's anger is associated with sadness because Cain recognizes that his goal of attaining God's favor is irretrievable; see Kruger, "A Cognitive Interpretation of Emotion of Anger in the Hebrew Bible," 182.
32 See also Gen 34:7. Some psychologists refer to the combination of anger and sadness as depression. In this vein, Westermann and Deurloo suggest that Cain's depression is experienced as an alienation from community ties. Westermann, *Genesis 1–11*, 297. See also Karel Deurloo, *Kain en Abel: Onderzoek naar exegetische methode in zake een "kleine literaire eenheid" in de Tenakh* (Amsterdam: Ten Have, 1967), 36.

8 Divine Ḥrh-Scripts in Old Poetry and in the Prophets

We discern three variants of the Broad-Biblical Ḥrh-Script in Old Poetry and Prophetic literature: the Divine Warrior Ḥrh-Script, the Synergistic Warrior Ḥrh-Script, and the Divine Kinsman Ḥrh-script. The scripts overlap with the Broad Biblical Ḥrh-Script in some ways while diverging from the broader model in various ways that appear aimed at conveying God's exceptional power.[1]

The Old Poetic and prophetic variants align with the Broad Biblical Ḥrh-Script in ascribing ḥrh to the more powerful party in an encounter. Notably, the variant scripts reserve this role for God. God, who is inherently more powerful than his target, is virtually always the typical subject of ḥrh in Old Poetic and prophetic texts.

The conceptual metaphor of ḥrh as heat, which is central to ḥrh more broadly, is also featured in the Old Poetic and prophetic scripts. However, in the latter's interpretation of the trait, ḥrh does not just heat its bearer, it manifests as a fiery substance that burns God's targets.

Interestingly, a prophetic and narrative variant overlaps in a notable way. As we saw, the tempered character of ḥrh toward kin is central to the concept in biblical narratives. Similarly, prophetic passages embed descriptions of God tempering his ḥrh within a kinship metaphor. Specifically, passages that describe God holding back and withdrawing his ḥrh are accompanied by descriptions of God and Israel as kin. The prophetic variant diverges from its narrative counterpart, however, in the outcome of this temperance. Human temperance at kin typically renders the angered party powerless to counter the disregard that provokes it. By contrast, in the Divine Kinsman Ḥrh-Script, God's temperance precipitates the return and repentance of his target.[2]

Divine Warrior Ḥrh-Script Represented by Exodus 15

Across Israel's Old Poetic literature, God is portrayed as a divine warrior who bests his cosmic enemies. It is not surprising, then, that this battle

DOI: 10.4324/9781003348719-8

theme is incorporated into the Old Poetic variant script. The script is as follows:

- God assaults the target with anger.
- Target is decimated.
- God asserts authority.

Exodus 15 offers a representative example of the Divine Warrior Ḥrh-Script (15:3–8):

יהוה איש מלחמה יהוה שמו: מרכבת פרעה וחילו ירה בים שלשיו טבעו בים-סוף: ימינך
יהוה נאדרי בכח ימינך יהוה תרעץ אויב: וברב גאונך תהרס קמיך תשלח חרנך יאכלמו
כקש: וברוח אפיך נערמו מים נצבו כמו נד נזלים קפאו תהמת בלב-ים:

The Divine-Warrior Ḥrh-Script, as represented by Exodus 15, overlaps with the Broad Biblical Ḥrh-Script in portraying ḥrh as a means of reasserting disregarded authority. It is in this vein that God is proclaimed king after overcoming Israel's enemies (יהוה ימלך לעלם, 15:18).

Anthropomorphic renderings of God's ḥrh simultaneously enhance an understanding of God by comparing the divine experience to one's own, while also expressing that God is exceptional. Terence Fretheim explains: "That the same terms are used for both human and divine ḥrh shows that God's ḥrh is considered analogous to that of human beings." Yet "in any assessment of such an 'anthropomorphic metaphor' for God, it is important to claim both a 'yes' and a 'no' with respect to the human analogue."[3]

This is clearly the case for the Divine Warrior Ḥrh-Script. This script, and Exodus 15 in particular, distinguishes itself in characterizing God's ḥrh as an element of battle—specifically, a material weapon. God is a "man of war" who comes to battle with a strong right arm (3–5) and with his ḥrh (6–7).[4] However, whereas Israel's human enemies hurl mere arrows and brandish mere swords in their arms, God hurls a far more potent weapon; his own ḥrh (ימינך יהוה תרעץ אויב: וברב גאונך תהרס קמיך תשלח חרנך יאכלמו כקש, 6b–7).[5]

The conceptual metaphor of God's ḥrh as heat is rendered similarly. The Old Poetic variant preserves the metaphor of burning ḥrh. However, in the broader script, ḥrh is felt as an internal burning; in this script, God's ḥrh materializes as fire that literally burns his enemies. In Exodus 15, God "devours" like "chaff" (תשלח חרנך יאכלמו כקש, 15:7). As the passage also describes God blowing his burning ḥrh like wind (וברוח אפיך נערמו מים, 15:8), the conceptual metaphor may be of a sea ravaged by the hot wind of a sirocco heat storm.[6]

On the surface, the targets of God's ḥrh in Exodus 15 are the Egyptians. However, this is not the full sense of the passage. Verse 4 states that the target of God's ḥrh burned like chaff, yet verse 7 relays that the Egyptians succumb to the sea, drowning under its weight (15:10). Moreover, the Egyptians are not actually named as the targets of God's ḥrh (15:7). Instead, God's wind, which blasts from his 'p alongside his ḥrh,[7] targets the sea (15:8). It would not be surprising that the sea was the target of God's ḥrh at some stage of the song's tradition history, since the motif of a storm god who bests the deity is prevalent throughout the ancient Near East. Regardless, in its current literary setting, embedded within the salvation history of the people of Israel, God's ḥrh conveys his overwhelming power to confront Israel's enemies and to reestablish himself as king over his people (יהוה ימלך לעלם, 15:18).

Synergistic Warrior Ḥrh-Script in Prophetic Texts

The characterization of God as a warrior and his ḥrh as a weapon of war is central to both Old Poetic and prophetic ḥrh-scripts. However, the character of this weapon differs among the collections. The Divine Warrior Ḥrh-Script of Old Poetry recalls the mythopoetic account of a solitary combatant who wields ḥrh as a weapon against his cosmic enemies. By contrast, the Synergistic Warrior Ḥrh-Script anticipates God battling alongside human armies, whose military assault is a realization of God's ḥrh. The Synergistic Warrior Ḥrh-Script is as follows:

- Target disregards God's authority.
- God assaults with anger that is realized in enemy assault.
- Target is decimated.
- God asserts authority.

A nuance of the Synergistic Warrior Ḥrh-Script is in its message that God's targets are to blame for their own suffering. The variant script conveys this by tethering the theme of God's ḥrh to the concrete reality of human warfare. Specifically, God's "arm of anger," "weapon of anger," and "armies of anger" are made manifest in the assaulting arms, weapons, and armies of Israel's enemies. Otherwise, God's ḥrh is linked, metonymically, with its own bitter consequences of war—specifically, the fires ignited by invading enemies and the spilled blood of those slain by the sword.[8]

Anger as a Human Army (Isaiah 10)

The expression of the Synergistic Warrior Ḥrh-Script in Isaiah 10 foregrounds the social dynamic of the dominant subject.[9] The passage portrays God as a mighty warrior who, in a reversal of the holy war motif, stretches out his arm to assault his own people with *'ap/z'm* (הוי אשור שבט אפי ומטה-הוא בידם זעמי, 10:5).[10]

Syntactically, *'ap/z'm* is in construct with "rod" and in apposition to "Assyria" (הוי אשור שבט אפי, 10:5a), as if to say that God's rod of *'ap/z'm* is the Assyrian army. Not only this: the rods that the Assyrian soldiers wield are also God's "rod of *z'm*" (ומטה-הוא בידם זעמי, 10:5b). As such, God's anger is not bound to the cosmic realm; God "sends an earthly enemy in place of natural forces and catastrophes to carry out the full consequences of his judgment."[11] As Göran Eidevall describes the setting, Assyria is an "(unwitting) instrument ... commissioned to carry out YHWH's punishment of Judah's northern neighbor states, in the aftermath of the Syro-Ephraimite crisis."[12] In short, the Assyrian assault *is* an assault of God's *'ap/z'm*.

Anger as Fires of War (Jeremiah 21)

Jeremiah 21's expression of the Synergistic Warrior *Ḥrh*-Script foregrounds the heat of God's *'p/ḥmh/qṣp*. Similar to Isaiah 10, where the Assyrian assault is, in fact, an assault of God's rod of *'ap/z'm*, in Jeremiah 21, the fires set by the invading army are a manifestation of God's *'p/ḥmh/qṣp* on earth (21:5–14):[13]

נלחמתי אני אתכם ביד נטויה ובזרוע חזקה ובאף ובחמה ובקצף גדול: והכיתי את-יושבי העיר הזאת ואת-האדם ואת-הבהמה בדבר גדול ומתו: ואחרי-כן נאם-יהוה אתן את-צדקיהו מלך-יהודה ואת-עבדיו ואת-העם ואת-הנשארים בעיר הזאת מן-הדבר מן-החרב ומן-הרעב ביד נבוכדראצר מלך-בבל וביד מבקשי נפשם והכם לפי-חרב לא-יחוס עליהם ולא יחמל ולא ירחם ... כי שמתי פני בעיר הזאת לרעה ולא לטובה נאם-יהוה ביד-מלך בבל תנתן ושרפה באש: ולבית מלך יהודה שמעו דבר-יהוה: בית דוד כה אמר יהוה דינו לבקר משפט והצילו גזול מיד עושק פן-תצא כאש חמתי ובערה ואין מכבה מפני רע מעלליהם: הנני אליך ישבת העמק צור המישר נאם-יהוה האמרים מי-יחת עלינו ומי יבוא במעונותינו: ופקדתי עליכם כפרי מעלליכם נאם-יהוה והצתי אש ביערה ואכלה כל-סביביה

God's burning *'p/ḥmh/qṣp* does not remain in the mythopoetic realm, such as it does in the Old Poetic script. Instead, it is manifest in the historical realities of Israel's bloody battles.[14] When God smites Israel with his mighty arm and with his *'p/ḥmh/qṣp*, the people succumb to the consequences of Nebuchadnezzar's military strike, which include famine, pestilence, and bloodshed (21:5–7).[15] When God unleashes his burning *'p/ḥmh/qṣp*, the people are burned by the fires set by the Babylonian king (21:10–14).[16]

By equating the fires of military invasion with the fire of God's *'p/ḥmh/qṣp*, the passage underscores that the people of Israel are responsible for their own suffering. They may have thought that Jerusalem was as impregnable as a steep valley, but by igniting God's *'p/ḥmh/qṣp*, they ignited the fires with which the Babylonian army burned down their city as if it were a forest (21:13–14).[17]

Anger as Blood Spilled in War

A trait that is central to the Synergistic Warrior *Ḥrh*-Script, though perhaps less so than the metaphors of anger as a fiery weapon of anger, is the metaphor of anger as a liquid that is either poured or filled in a cup. Some passages imply, at least initially, that God's anger materializes as wine.[18] Jeremiah says this explicitly when he describes "the cup of wine of anger" (25:15–16):

כי כה אמר יהוה אלהי ישראל אלי קח את-כוס היין החמה הזאת מידי והשקיתה אתו את-כל-הגוים אשר אנכי שלח אותך אליהם: ושתו והתגעשו והתהללו מפני החרב אשר אנכי שלח בינתם:

Both Jeremiah and Second Isaiah warn that when the people drink from God's cup of anger,[19] that is, from the "dregs of the bowl of staggering," they stagger, vomit, and fall down faint and drunk:

כה-אמר יהוה צבאות אלהי ישראל שתו ושכרו וקיו ונפלו ולא תקומו מפני החרב אשר אנכי שלח ביניכם: והיה כי ימאנו לקחת-הכוס מידך לשתות ואמרת אליהם כה אמר יהוה צבאות שתו ותשתו:
Jer 25:27–28

שתים הנה קראתיך מי ינוד לך והשד והשבר והרעב והחרב מי אנחמך: בניך עלפו שכבו בראש כל-חוצות כתוא מכמר המלאים חמת-יהוה גערת אלהיך: לכן שמעי-נא זאת עניה ושכרת ולא מיין: כי-אמר אדניך ואלהיך יריב עמו הנה לקחתי מידך את-כוס התרעלה את-קבעת כוס חמתי לא-תוסיפי לשתותה עוד:
Isa 51:19–22

And yet, they qualify that the fallen drinkers only *appear* to be drunk with wine. In reality, they have succumbed to the disasters of war. The people lie on the streets not because they are passed out drunk but because they have endured famine. They stagger, vomit, and rise no more—not from drunkenness but because they have been felled by the sword. More broadly, drunkenness is a metaphor for death, and the people who drink from God's cup of *ḥmh* have died in war.

The context of war and death suggests that the substance of God's *ḥmh*, which resembles wine and fills God's cup, is conceived as blood.[20] The people's blood, which is spilled when God assaults with anger, is the liquid embodiment of this *ḥmh*. The Prophets may imagine that the people's own blood is poured upon them or that they are forced to drink from it as a ritual acknowledgment that by incurring God's *ḥmh* through sin, they have poured their own blood.[21] In other words, their deaths are on their own hands.

Divine Kinsman Ḥrh-Script

The Divine Kinsman Ḥrh-Script prevalent in prophetic literature overlaps with the Kin-Targeted Ḥrh-Script of biblical narratives in their portrayal of the tempering power of kinship. The Divine Kinsman Ḥrh-Script is as follows:[22]

- Israel disregards God's authority.
- God punishes Israel.
- God's anger turns.
- Israel repents.

As we have seen, in biblical narratives, ḥrh is tempered by kinship, and not reprisal or recompense. Here, as well, God turns away his anger at his "wife" and "child" absent prior repentance.[23]

Nonetheless, the human and divine ḥrh scripts differ in outcomes. In biblical narratives, anger at kin, which is typically blunted by affection and self-interest, is ineffectual at restoring authority. By contrast, in the books of the Prophets, God's temperance is followed by Israel's acknowledgment of his authority and their repentance, at least for a time.

Hosea 11[24]

Hosea 11 introduces God as a father who loves, rears, and nurtures Israel, his adopted son:

- God loves or cares for his son Israel.
- God delivers Israel into the devouring swords of Egypt and Assyria.
- God withholds anger.
- Israel returns to God.

Verses 1–6 make the case for divine ḥrh. The people of Israel, characterized as God's son, reject God, their father, and instead rely on Baalim. When they refuse to repent, God delivers them into the hands of Egypt and the swords of Assyria (11:3–6).

Notably, God's ḥrh is cited neither in Hosea's account of Israel's sins nor amid God's punitive response.[25] God's ḥrh is cited only later, in a description of why God does *not* execute it (11:1–9).[26]

כי נער ישראל ואהבהו וממצרים קראתי לבני: קראו להם כן הלכו מפניהם לבעלים יזבחו
ולפסלים וקטרון: ואנכי תרגלתי לאפרים קחם על-זרועתיו ולא ידעו כי רפאתים: בחבלי
אדם אמשכם בעבתות אהבה ואהיה להם כמרימי על על לחיהם ואט אליו אוכיל: לא ישוב
אל-ארץ מצרים ואשור הוא מלכו כי מאנו לשוב: וחלה חרב בעריו וכלתה בדיו ואכלה

ממעצבותיהם: ועמי תלואים למשובתי ואל על יקראהו יחד לא ירוממו: איך אתנך אפרים
אמגנך ישראל איך אתנך כאדמה אשימך כצבאים נהפך עלי לבי יחד נכמרו נחומי: לא
אעשה חרון אפי לא אשוב לשחת אפרים כי אל אנכי ולא-איש בקרבך קדוש ולא אבוא
בעיר

The passage offers no indication that the people have repented. In fact, nothing appears to have transpired between verses 6–7 and verses 8–9 that would explain God's change of attitude.[27]

What does appear to influence God's temperance is paternal love (11:2, 4), for God is overcome with compassion נכמרו נחומי (11:8). Similar to how this phrase is used elsewhere—to describe affection that precipitates a compassionate act toward kin—here, too, the phrase describes God's compassion overwhelming any act of anger at his beloved son.[28]

However, the Divine Kinsman *Ḥrh*-Script diverges from the Kin-Targeted *Ḥrh*-Script in a significant way. Rather than being weak and ineffectual, such as kin-targeted *ḥrh* is portrayed, God's forbearance is rhetorical. Macintosh explains: "The harshness of Yahweh's judgment is designed to provoke penitence and piety. Man punishes to destroy: God intervenes for the purpose of correction (after Jerome). Accordingly, Yahweh will not turn back to destroy his nation."[29] Indeed, God's choice not to "do" *ḥrh* ultimately facilitates the renewal of his patriarchy, as it persuades Israel to return to God (אחרי יהוה ילכו, 11:10) so that God may return the people to their land (והושבתים על בתיהם, 11:11).[30]

Notes

1 The root *ḥrh*, which is so pervasive across biblical narratives, is rarer in Old Poetry and in the Prophets. These collections tend to prefer, instead, *'ap*, *ḥmh*, *qṣp* and *z'm*, to connote a response to disregarded authority that can precipitate aggressive actions. The preference for these roots, coupled with the fact that translators tend to equate them with "anger," leads us to widen the scope of our study to include these roots in our survey of Old Poetic and prophetic scripts. Nonetheless, since their meanings accord broadly with the meaning of the term *ḥrh*, we will stick with the use of the root *ḥrh* to describe the scripts that they anticipate. See also Chapter 7 fn. 17.

2 For example, Deuteronomy 32, focuses attention on God's destructiveness; in Psalm 18, it foregrounds God's role as deliverer.

3 Terence Fretheim, "Theological Reflections of the Wrath of God in the Old Testament," *Horizons in Biblical Theology* 24/2 (2002): 6.

4 For a discussion of characterizations of God possessing a human body, see Esther Hamori, *When Gods Were Men: The Embodied God in Biblical and Near Eastern Literature* (Berlin: De Gruyter, 2008). The *piel* form of the root *šlḥ* in v. 7 underscores the militaristic force that propels Yahweh's arm, like a warrior hurls arrows; see Ps 80:12. In ancient Near Eastern mythological traditions, as reflected in both texts and monumental representations, storm deities can carry lightning as their weapons. Delbert Hillers, "Amos 7:4 and Ancient Parallels," *Catholic Biblical Quarterly* 26/2 (1964): 223.

88 Divine Ḥrh-Scripts in Old Poetry and in the Prophets

5   Further examples of *ḥrh* as a divine weapon include Ps 18:7–17 (=2 Sam 22:8: 8–16); Hab 3:8–9.
6   Chaff is evaporated by wind in Isa 40:24; Jer 13:24; Ps 83:13. It is also burned by fire in Isa 5:24; 33:11; 47:14; Obad 1:18; Joel 2:5; Mal 3:13; Job 41:20. Fitzgerald suggests that, in this passage, God's *ḥrh* is imagined as an element of a sirocco-breathing deity coming in that storm; Aloysius Fitzgerald, *The Lord of the East Wind* (Washington, D.C.: CBA, 2002), 151–52. This is in keeping with a number of psalms that witness Yahweh's devouring fire within his theophanic storm (Ps 29:7; 56:3; 83:15; 97:3).
7   In this case, the verse chooses the form חרון.
8   For more examples of God's *ḥrh* manifest in enemy armies, see Isa 5:25–30; 9:7–10:4; 13:3–6; Jer 50:25; 21:5–7; Ezek 25:13–15.
9   Isaiah 10 opens with a description of God hurling '*p*—presumably, with his still-outstretched arm. The refrain בכל זאת לא שב אפו ועוד ידו נטויה is the last in a series of refrains that explain the recurring assaults against Israel (Isa 9:11, 16, 20; 10:4–5).
10 See Ch. 7 fn. 17 on the diverse anger terms.
11 Wildberger attributes this change to the waning of mythological thought; Hans Wildberger, *Isaiah 1–12* (Minneapolis: Fortress, 1991), 417.
12 Göran Eidevall, *Prophecy and Propaganda: Images of Enemies in the Book of Isaiah* (Winona Lake, Ind.: Eisenbrauns, 2009), 48.
13 Miller observes: "Yahweh's devouring fire seems to be predominantly expressive of the divine warrior's wrath and destruction," particularly within the "prophetic imagination and especially in the motifs of holy war." Patrick Miller, "Fire in the Mythology of Canaan and Israel," in *Israelite Religion and Biblical Theology: Collected Essays*. (Sheffield: Sheffield Academic Press, 2000), 21.
14 When a conceptual metaphor gains traction, it may lose the meaning that it originally possessed; see Ronald R. Butters, "Do 'Conceptual Metaphors' Really Exist?" *Southeastern Conference on Linguistics Bulletin* 5/3 (1981): 108–17, esp. 111, 115. The metaphor of poured *ḥmh* as poured blood may remain salient only in the context of battle.
15 E.g., Jer 14:12–15; 16:4; 32:36; 44:12, 18, 27.
16 Fire is a pervasive motif throughout Jeremiah, most frequently describing a divine fire that emanates from the deity or real-life fires ignited by Nebuchadnezzar that burn Judah and Jerusalem (see Jeremiah 4 and 7). Other prophetic passages link God's fiery *ḥrh* to actual fires of war as well. In Isaiah 30, the fire that God wields on the mythological plane punishes the Assyrian king on the historical plane (30:27–33). In Isaiah 66, those who succumb to the divine warrior's fiery *ḥrh*/*ḥmh* appear to be victims of war (66:22–24). In Jeremiah and Ezekiel, God's *ḥrh*/*ḥmh* arises in his nostrils as fire and rains down upon the people a storm of hailstones and fire, which are contextualized within an invasion (Jer 15:14; Ezek 13:13; 16:41–42; 21:31; 22:20–21; 38:18–23). Other passages that link God's divine fire to the fires of war include Num 21:27–30; Isa 34:1–10; Amos 1–2; Micah 1–3; Zechariah 12; Joel 1, 2, and 4.
17 For a similar description see 7:20. McKane explains, on this passage, "Yahweh's anger is envisaged as a fire which, once ignited, defies all efforts to extinguish it. The fire of his judgment burns until everything is destroyed"; William A. McKane, *Critical and Exegetical Commentary on Jeremiah* (London: Bloomsbury Academic, 2000), 510. I.e., once ignited, the fire of God's *ḥrh*/ḥmh does not discriminate among its victims, burning every tree and all the fruits in its path.

18 There has been much debate over the *Sitz im Leben* of this image, and no consensus has emerged to explain why the Prophets identify this substance—at least initially—as wine. A history of the debate is provided in Deena Grant, "A Brief Discussion of the Difference between Human and Divine חמה," *Biblica* 91 (2020): 422n17.

19 This may evoke the ordeal of drinking from the bitter waters, which the accused adulteress must undergo (Num 5:19–25). In both contexts, the offenders are compelled to consume a liquid that represents their offense. The analogy to an adulteress's punishment is especially pertinent to Jeremiah, who repeatedly compares Israel to an adulterous wife (Jer 2:20; 3:1, 3, 6, 8; 5:7).

20 Blood is the substance most frequently poured in the Bible. Additionally, drinking from a cup is linked to punishment (Jer 49:12; Ezek 23:31–32; Ps 11:6; 75:8; Lam 34:21; 51:7) and is particularly linked to being felled by the sword (Jer 46:10). McKane entertains the possibility that the content of Yahweh's cup of *ḥmh* in Jeremiah 25 represents blood, but he cautions that "this association of the flowing of the juice of the grape and the shedding of blood (in Isaiah 63) does not help us when we encounter ... wine [that] is contained in a cup or chalice and is offered, as if by a host, to assembled guests; see McKane, *A Critical and Exegetical Commentary on Jeremiah*, 488. He concludes, therefore: "It is, probably, best not to pursue any one interpretation of the 'cup of wrath' passages too obsessively with a view to excluding all other possibilities"; ibid., 389. The linkage of wine and blood is supported in a number of passages. Blood is described as inebriating (Deut 32:4), and harvested vines are associated with slaughter (6:9; Judg 20:44–46). See Robert M. Good, "Metaphorical Gleanings from Ugarit," *JJS* 33 (1982): 54–59.

21 Grant, "A Brief Discussion of the Difference between Human and Divine חמה," 423. This interpretation is supported by Isa 63:2–6, where winemaking is a metaphor for God's punitive *ḥmh* and wine is a metaphor for blood. When God treads a winepress with his *ḥmh*, the juice of the grapes sprays (נצח) his robes red; when God tramples his people in *ḥmh*, their lifeblood pours (נצחם) to the earth. In Ezek 21:36–37, the Babylonian invasion is described, metaphorically, as an event of burning metal, with Israel as the metal and the Babylonians as the metalworkers. When God pours/blows his fiery *ḥmh* upon the metal, i.e., upon Israel, they are delivered into the hands of metalworkers, i.e., to the Babylonians. The liquification of the metal with heat by metalworkers may stand for the blood of the people, which is poured as a consequence of enemy invasion. The consequence of God's poured blood comes to stand metonymically for it; see also Ezekiel's use of the same root, נתכ, to describe the melting of metal into liquid via God's blowing his fiery *ḥmh* in 22:20–2.

22 God adopts Israel as a "son" and as a "daughter," and he is called "father" (e.g., Ezek 16:4–7; Hos 11:1; 14:4–5). He enters into a marriage covenant with her and is called "husband" (e.g., Ezek 16:8; Hosea 1–10). Their relationship is characterized by love (*'hb* in Deut 4:37; Hos 8:5–9; 11:34), loyalty (*ḥsd* in Exod 15:13; Deut 5:10; 7:9; Isa 54:8; Ps 86:5), and fidelity (*'mt* in Hos 11:1; Ezek 16:8; Ps 89:29–30; 132:1–2), characteristics that typically define human kin relations. God's role as patriarch is reflected also in his bequeathing of his heritage, the land of Canaan, to his people (Gen 12:1; 15:17; Deut 3:18; 5:16). Frank Moore Cross, *From Epic to Canon: History and Literature in Ancient Israel* (Baltimore: Johns Hopkins University Press, 2000), 5–7.

23 Other examples of God tempering his *ḥrh* at Israel are Jer 33:5; Isa 54:8; 57:17; 64:4. See also Jeremiah 2–3.
24 See Hos 11:9; 14:5 (*ḥrh* is also cited in Hos 5:10; 8:5; 11:9; 13:11, 14; 14:5).
25 There is some argument regarding how to interpret the role of divine *ḥrh* here, with a major interpretive question revolving around whether לא אעשה חרון אפי describes God's justifying or restraining his *ḥrh* at his son. Interpreting the twice-stated *lō'* asseveratively, Andersen and Freedman understand the verse as describing God's determination to kill, despite his previous hesitation. Though he is loath to hurt them, he asserts: "I will certainly act out my burning *ḥrh*. I will certainly come back to destroy Ephraim." Francis I. Andersen and David Noel Freedman, *Hosea: A New Translation with Introduction and Commentary* (New York: Doubleday, 1980), 588. Interpreting the two *lō'* phrases as a series of negative statements that describe God's restraint of *ḥrh*, Wolff sees the verse as a reassurance that God will not revoke his redemptive actions, thus translating: "I will not execute my *ḥrh*, I will not turn and devastate Ephraim." Hans Walter Wolff, *Hosea: A Commentary on the Book of the Prophet Hosea* (Minneapolis: Fortress, 1974), 72. Macintosh similarly translates: "I will not give effect to my fierce *ḥrh*, nor will I turn back to destroy Ephraim"; Andrew A. Macintosh, *Hosea: A Critical and Exegetical Commentary* (Edinburgh: T&T Clark, 1997), 464.
26 The description of God calling his son out of Egypt represents his adoption of Israel. Adoption, as opposed to birthing, allows God to be the sole parent while retaining his male identity. For more on adoption imagery, see Janet Melnyk, "When Israel Was a Child: Ancient Near Eastern Adoption Formulas and the Relationship between God and Israel," in *History and Interpretation: Essays in Honor of John H. Hayes*, ed. M. Patrick Graham, William P. Brown, and Jeffrey Kuan (Sheffield: Sheffield Academic Press, 1993), 245–59. The term תרגלתי, "rear," is a hapax legomenon whose precise meaning is uncertain. In addition to providing a history of its interpretation, Hutton and Marzouk provide a history of its interpretation; Jeremy M. Hutton and Safwat Marzouk, "The Morphology of the tG-Stem in Hebrew and Tirgaltî Hos 11:3," *Journal of Hebrew Scriptures* 12 (2012): 2.
27 Macintosh dates this passage to 724, when Shalmaneser V occupied the majority of Ephraim and captured Hosea, but left Samaria unconquered; see Macintosh, *Hosea*, 454. Others suggest that the passage precedes the capture of Hosea and the beginning of the siege of Samaria. For a discussion of the proposed historical contexts, see Ehud Ben Zvi, *Hosea* (Grand Rapids, Mich.: Eerdmans, 2005), 238.
28 The root *nḥm* may underscore this point, for it "is not linked to forgiveness but is grounded in the weakness of the people who could not survive the punishment"; see Besel H. Simian-Yofre and Heinz-Josef Fabry, "נחם *nḥm*," *TDOT* 9:347.
29 Macintosh, *Hosea*, 465.
30 Whether or not these verses were added after the fall of Northern Israel as a rhetorical means to coerce the exiles in Assyria and Egypt to return to their homeland, they portray God's restraint of *ḥrh* yielding a renewed bond with his people. Wolff, *Hosea*, 197–202. For another example, see Hos 14:4–5.

9 Conclusion

Biblical translators virtually always interpret *snʾ* as hate and *ḥrh* as anger. But just how equivalent are these ancient Hebrew and modern English terms are? This is the question we took up in this book.

For an answer, we turned to the field of cognitive linguistics, which aims to understand how knowledge is conceived and organized, as revealed by language. Cognitive linguists argue that concepts are identified on the basis of "best example"—prototypes. People conjure a "best example," and they judge a potential instance based on how well it resembles the prototype. Cognitive linguists also posit that some prototypes, including emotion prototypes, are organized sequentially in a script-like fashion.

Where do emotions-scripts come from? Researchers have well established that people raised in different cultures can possess profoundly different ideas and beliefs about emotions. A famous example of this was documented in the 1960s by Jean Briggs, who engaged in fieldwork with a group of Canadian Inuits. As Briggs settled into life with her host family, she became increasingly aware that her hosts had begun relating to her as if she were a stubborn and irritating child. And they did so while remaining outwardly welcoming and polite. She noticed, as well, that the entire Utku community began to ignore her. What was she doing wrong?[1]

Eventually, Briggs came to the conclusion that she was looked down in the eyes of the Utku because she conceptualized emotions differently from the way they did. An American anthropologist, Briggs was used to expressing her emotions. For the Utku, however, emotional control was a highly valued trait, referred to as *ihuma*. "One rule governing all Utku behavior was that one should never become angry."[2] In fact, "the avoidance of expressions of extreme emotion, above all anger, was central to the Utku sense of self." Troublesome thoughts were even believed to make someone ill.[3]

As the Utku understand it, *ihuma* can take time to emerge in children, but it is acquired by adulthood. This is why Briggs's host

DOI: 10.4324/9781003348719-9

family comfortably tolerated their baby's crying and screaming but found Briggs's expressive temperament to be unpalatable. Briggs was an adult with a fully formed *ihuma*. Yet she was unable to communicate, regulate, and manage hostile emotions with the type of emotional control and absence of anger that governed Utku identity.[4] Briefly put, the Utku experienced anger, but they conceived of it differently from the way Briggs did:

> The control required was much greater than that to which I was accustomed to discipline myself. At the same time, I was under considerably greater strain than I was used to, and the resulting tensions pressed for expression. Though I did my best to express them through laughter, as Utku did, laughter did not come naturally.... There was the coldness in my voice which concealed a desire to weep with fatigue or a frustration when I had to say for the thousandth time: I don't understand. There was the time when hurrying to leave the iglu, I unthinkingly moved Raigili aside with my hand instead of quietly telling her to move. There were the critical remarks I murmured in English ... the burst of profanity.[5]

Although the intense feelings of the Utku were successfully suppressed, Briggs's feelings of frustration and anger would find ways to get out.[6]

Briggs did not recognize her hosts' disapproval immediately, likely because of their generous responses to her outbursts and their acceptances of her apologies. These responses, however, were socially appropriate expressions of her hosts' own *ihuma*. They did not reflect actual warm feelings.

The type of control encountered, and unsuccessfully borne by Briggs, may be characteristic of emotion concepts across a number of Eastern cultures. It has been suggested that in Western cultures that impute high value on the independent self, displays of anger are regarded more positively than in Eastern cultures that put greater value on belongingness to the group. Although in one culture, responding to an indignity with expressed anger may be well regarded and even applauded as a justified sign of self-worth, in another culture, displays of anger may be perceived as not worth the negative interpersonal consequences that can come from them. Disapproving onlookers might wonder, "Why do you threaten the cohesion of the entire group over a personal slight?"[7]

As an ancient work, the Bible stands, relative to us, at a far greater cultural divide than stood between Briggs and the Utku. As such, it is undeniable that biblical emotion terms bore very different scripts and evoked very different networks of cognitive associations. This has some interesting theological implications. I offer an example:

theologians and scholars alike have long grappled with how to interpret Deut 6:5: ואהבת את יהוה אלהיך בכל-לבבך ובכל נפשך ובכל מאדך. Biblical translators and interpreters virtually always translate the term *'hb* as "love." But how can God command people to feel an emotion? Is this even possible? And if it is not possible, what does Deuteronomy demand of Israel?

In an early reckoning with the possibility that ancient Hebrew emotion terms do not precisely accord with modern English ones, William Moran argued that the meaning of *'ahb* may be better understood if we consider it against the background of contemporaneous literature.[8] Moran points out that love is commanded, for example, in another ancient Near Eastern first-millennium text. In order to ensure loyalty to his son and successor, the Assyrian king Esarhaddon demands of his vassals: "You will love as yourselves Ashurbanipal," and he threatens harsh punishments upon those who do not do so.[9] Many agree that this love, which Esarhaddon demands of his vassals, is not affective love. Instead, it is treaty language that connotes political loyalty.

Does the command to love God in the book of Deuteronomy have a similar sense? Perhaps. I would argue that, at the very least, obedience to a treaty is more salient to the idealized model of *'hb* than it is to the concept represented by the modern English term "love."

In a similar vein, we cannot presume to understand the full sense of *sn'* and *ḥrh* simply because we know the definitions of hate and anger. This is why we must attempt to interpret their meanings on their own terms, by laying bare the culturally distinct sequences of traits that make up their prototypical scripts.

To broadly recap some of our findings, both the Broad Biblical *Sn'*-Script and the Broad Biblical *Ḥrh*-Script connote a socially dominant subject who targets another for aggressive action. The centrality of social dominance, in these scripts, suggests that *sn'* and *ḥrh* are distinct from English hate and anger, in that they communicate a privileged social status.

Identifying the widest range of traits that make up *sn'*- and *ḥrh*-scripts has allowed us to discern the ways biblical narratives, poetry, and prophetic literature both conform with and diverge from the broader emotion-scripts toward diverse aims. We have observed that narrative variants of *sn'*- and *ḥrh*-scripts encourage a more nuanced view of the bearers of these emotions. In biblical narratives, *sn'*-scripts focus on the moral standing of the hater, and *ḥrh*-scripts direct attention to the legitimacy of the subject's authority. For example, we have observed that poetic and prophetic variants of *sn'*- and *ḥrh*-scripts also focus on morality and dominance, but they do so toward the narrower aim of portraying God as exceptionally righteous and dominant.

In summary, all human beings, across time and space, experience emotions. However, not all dimensions of the emotional experience are shared. All of us experience the world through our physical bodies, but when, why, and how our bodies experience emotions are mediated by an indeterminate network of socially constructed and culturally bound cognitive and affective associations.

Notes

1 J. Plamper, *The History of Emotions* (Oxford: Oxford University Press, 2015) 90–95. Citing extensively from Jean Briggs, *Never in Anger: Portrait of an Eskimo Family* (Cambridge, MA: Harvard University Press, 1970).
2 Plamper, *The History of Emotions*, 91.
3 Plamper, *The History of Emotions*, 94.
4 Plamper, *The History of Emotions*, 92.
5 Plamper, *The History of Emotions*, 93–94.
6 Plamper, *The History of Emotions*, 93.
7 For a discussion and sources, refer to Jiyoung Park and Shinobu Kitayama, "Anger, Expression and Health: The Cultural Moderation Hypothesis," in *The Oxford Handbook of Integrative Health Science*, ed. Carol D. Ryff and Robert F. Krueger (New York: Oxford University Press, 2018), 384.
8 Moran, "The Ancient Near Eastern Background of the Love of God in Deuteronomy."
9 Moran, "The Ancient Near Eastern Background of the Love of God in Deuteronomy," 80.

Bibliography

Allen, Leslie C. *Ezekiel 1–19*. Nashville: Thomas Nelson, 1994.
———. *Jeremiah: A Commentary*. Louisville: Westminster John Knox, 2008.
Andersen, Francis I., and David Noel Freedman. *Hosea: A New Translation with Introduction and Commentary*. Garden City: Doubleday, 1980.
Aster, Shawn Zelig. *The Unbeatable Light: Melammu and Its Biblical Parallels*. Münster: Ugarit, 2012.
Averill, James. *Anger and Aggression: An Essay on an Emotion*. New York: Springer, 1982.
Baloian, Bruce Edward. *Anger in the Old Testament*. New York: Peter Lang, 1992.
Beck, Aaron. *Prisoners of Hate: The Cognitive Basis of Anger, Hostility, and Violence*. New York: HarperCollins, 1999.
Ben-Ze'ev, Aaron. *The Subtlety of Emotions*. Cambridge: MIT Press, 2000.
Ben Zvi, Ehud. *Hosea*. Grand Rapids: Eerdmans, 2005.
Berlin, Adele. *Esther: The Traditional Hebrew Text with the New JPS Translation*. Philadelphia: Jewish Publication Society, 2001.
Botterweck, G. Johannes. "חרה *ḥārâ*." *Theological Dictionary of the Old Testament*. 5 (1986): 171–5.
Branson, Robert. "The Polyvalent *sn'*: An Emotional, Performative, and Covenantal Term." *Biblical Research* 51 (2007): 5–15.
Brice, Gene. "A Study of Hate and Anger in Old Testament Man." Ph.D. diss., Yale University, 1962.
Briggs, Jean. *Never in Anger: Portrait of an Eskimo Family*. Cambridge: Harvard University Press, 1970.
Brogaard, Berit. *Hatred: Understanding Our Most Dangerous Emotion*. New York: Oxford, 2020.
Brown, William. *Psalms*. Nashville: Abingdon, 2010.
Brueggemann, Walter. *The Theology of the Book of Jeremiah*. Cambridge: Cambridge University, 2007.
Butters, Ronald R. "Do 'Conceptual Metaphors' Really Exist?" *Southeastern Conference on Linguistics Bulletin* 5/3 (1981): 108–17.
Clifford, Richard J. *The Creation Accounts in the ANE and in the Bible*. Washington D.C: Catholic Biblical Association, 1994.
Clore, Gerald, and Andrew Ortony. "What More Is There to Emotional Concepts than Prototypes?" *Journal of Personality and Social Psychology* (1991): 48–50.

Clore, Gerald, et al. "Where Does Anger Dwell?" In *Perspectives on Anger and Emotion*, 1–46. Ed. Robert. S. Wryer, Jr. and Thomas K. Skrull. Hillsdale, N.J.: Lawrence Erlbaum, 1993.

Collins, John Joseph, Frank M. Cross, and Adela Yarbro Collins. *Daniel: A Commentary on the Book of Daniel*. Minneapolis: Augsburg Fortress, 1993.

Cross, Frank Moore. *Canaanite Myth and the Hebrew Epic: Essays in the History of the Religion of Israel*. Cambridge: Harvard University Press, 1987.

_____. *From Epic to Canon: History and Literature in Ancient Israel*. Baltimore: Johns Hopkins University Press, 2000.

Davitz, Joel Robert. *The Language of Emotion*. New York: Academic Press, 1969.

Day, Peggy. "Adulterous Jerusalem's Imagined Demise: Death of a Metaphor in Ezekiel XVI." *VT* 50 (2000): 286–304.

Deurloo, Karel. *Kain en Abel: Onderzoek naar exegetische methode in zake een 'kleine literaire eenheid' in de Tenakh*. Amsterdam: Ten Have, 1967.

DeVries, Simon. "Remembrance in Ezekiel: A Study of an Old Testament Theme." *Interpretation* 16 (1962): 58–64.

Eidevall, Göran. *Amos: A New Translation with Introduction and Commentary*. New Haven: Yale University Press, 2017.

_____. *Prophecy and Propaganda: Images of Enemies in the Book of Isaiah*. Winona Lake, Ind: Eisenbrauns, 2009.

_____. "Rejected Sacrifice in the Prophetic Literature: A Rhetorical Perspective." *Svensk Exegetisk Årsbok* 78 (2013): 31–45.

Ekman, Paul. *Emotions Revealed: Recognizing Faces and Feelings to Improve Communication and Emotional Life*. 2nd ed. New York: Henry Holt, 2003.

Fehr, Beverly, and Mark Baldwin. "Prototype and Script Analysis of Laypeople's Knowledge of Anger." In *Knowledge Structures in Close Relationships: A Social Psychological Approach*. Ed. Gary Fletcher and Julie Fitness. New York: Psychology Press, 1996.

Fischer, Agneta, Antony Manstead, and Patricia Rodriguez Mosquera. "The Role of Honour-Related vs. Individualistic Values in Conceptualizing Pride, Shame, and Anger: Spanish and Dutch Cultural Prototypes." *Cognition and Emotion* 13/2 (1999): 149–79.

Fitness, Julie. "Anger in the Workplace: An Emotion Script Approach to Anger Episodes between Workers and Their Superiors, Coworkers, and Subordinates." *Journal of Organizational Behavior*. Supp. Special Issue 21 (2000): 147–62.

_____, and Garth J. O. Fletcher. "Love, Hate, Anger, and Jealousy in Close Relationships: A Prototype and Cognitive Appraisal Analysis." *Journal of Personality and Social Psychology* 65/5 (1993): 942–58.

Fitzgerald, Aloysius. *The Lord of the East Wind*. Washington DC: Catholic Biblical Association, 2002.

Fitzmyer, Joseph. "A Note on Ez 16:30." *CBQ* 23 (1961): 460–62.

Fletcher, Julie, and Garth J.O. Fletcher. "Love, Hate, Anger, and Jealousy in Close Relationships: A Prototype and Cognitive Appraisal Analysis." *Journal of Personality and Social Psychology* 65/6 (1993): 942–58.

Fretheim, Terence. "Theological Reflections of the Wrath of God in the Old Testament." *Horizons in Biblical Theology* 24/2 (2002): 1–26.

Frijda, Nico J. *The Emotions*. New York: Cambridge, 1986.

Galambush, Julie. *Jerusalem in the Book of Ezekiel: The City as Yahweh's Wife*. Cambridge: Scholars Press, 1992.
Gaylin, William. *The Rage Within*. New York: Simon and Schuster, 1984.
Giuseppe, Raymond, and Jeffrey Froh. "What Cognitions Predict State Anger?" *Journal of Rational-Emotive and Cognitive-Behavior Therapy* 20 (2002): 133–50.
Goldin, Judah. "The Youngest Son or Where Does Genesis 38 Belong?" *Journal of Biblical Literature* 96 (1977): 27–44.
Goldingay, John. *Daniel*. Dallas: Word Books, 1989.
Good, Robert M. "Metaphorical Gleanings from Ugarit." *JJS* 33 (1982): 54–59.
Grant, Deena. *Divine Anger in the Hebrew Bible*. Washington, DC: Catholic Biblical Association, 2014.
_____, "A Brief Discussion of the Difference between Human and Divine חמה." *Biblica* (2010): 418–24.
Greenberg, Moshe. *Ezekiel 1–20: A New Translation with Introduction and Commentary*. Garden City: Doubleday, 1983.
Gregg, Melissa, and Gregory Seigworth. Ed. *The Affect Theory Reader*. Durham: Duke University Press, 2010.
Griffiths, Paul. *What Emotions Really Are: The Problem of Psychological Categories*. Chicago: University of Chicago Press, 1997.
Gruber, Mayer. "The Tragedy of Cain and Abel: A Case of Depression." *Jewish Quarterly Review* 69 (1978): 89–97.
Guenther, Allen. "A Typology of Israelite Marriage: Kinship, Socio-Economic and Religious Factors." *Journal for the Study of the Old Testament* 29 (2005): 387–407.
Hamori, Esther. *When Gods Were Men: The Embodied God in Biblical and Near Eastern Literature*. Berlin: De Gruyter, 2008.
Heine, Bernd. "The Body in Language: Observations from Grammaticalization." In *The Body in Language: Comparative Studies of Linguistic Embodiment*. Ed. Matthias Brenzinger and Iwona Kraska-Szlenk. Leiden: Brill, 2014.
Hillers, Delbert R "Some Performative Utterances in the Bible." In *Poets before Homer: Collected Essays on Ancient Literature*. Ed. Dobbs-Allsopp. Winona Lake: Eisenbrauns, 2015.
_____. "Amos 7:4 and Ancient Parallels." *Catholic Biblical Quarterly* 26/2 (1964): 221–25.
Holladay, William L. *The Architecture of Jeremiah 1–20*. Plainsboro: Associated University Press, 1976.
Huffmon, Herbert. "The Covenant Lawsuit in the Prophets." *Journal of Biblical Literature* 78/4 (1959): 285–95.
Hugenberger, Gordon Paul. *Marriage as a Covenant: A Study of Biblical Law and Ethics Governing Marriage Developed from the Perspective of Malachi*. Leiden: Brill, 1993.
Longacre, Robert. *Joseph: A Story of Divine Providence, a Text Theoretical and Textlinguistic Analysis of Genesis 37 and 39–48*. Winona Lake: Eisenbrauns, 2003.
Hutton, Jeremy, and Safwat Marzouk. "The Morphology of the tG-Stem in Hebrew and Tirgaltî in Hos 11:3." *Journal of Hebrew Scriptures* 12 (2012): 1–41.

Bibliography

Hyman, Ronald T. "Final Judgment: The Ambiguous Moral Question That Culminates Genesis 34," *Jewish Bible Quarterly* 28 (2000): 93–101.

Izzard, Carol. *The Face of Emotion*. New York: Appleton-Century-Crofts, 1971.

Joo, Samantha. *Provocation and Punishment: The Anger of God in the Book of Jeremiah and Deuteronomistic Theology*. Berlin: De Gruyter, 2006.

Kang, Sa-Moon. *Divine War in the Old Testament and in the Ancient Near East*. Berlin: De Gruyter, 1989.

Klein, Ralph. *Ezekiel: The Prophet and His Message*. Columbia: University of South Carolina Press, 1988.

_____. *1 Samuel*. Nashville: Thomas Nelson, 1983.

Kottsieper, Ingo. "We Have a Little Sister." In *Families and Family Relations as Represented in Early Judaisms and Early Christianities: Texts and Fictions*, 49–80. Ed. Athalya Brenner and Jan Willem van Henten. Leiderdorp: Deo, 2000.

Kövecses, Zoltán. *Metaphor and Emotion: Language, Culture, and Body in Human Feeling*. New York: Cambridge University Press, 2003.

_____. "The Concept of Anger: Universal or Culture Specific." *Psychopathology* 33/4 (2000): 159–70.

_____. *Metaphors of Anger, Pride, and Love: A Lexical Approach to the Structure of Concepts*. Amsterdam: John Benjamins, 1986.

Kruger, Paul A. "A Cognitive Interpretation of the Emotion of Anger in the Hebrew Bible." *Journal of North-West Semitic Languages* 26/1 (2000): 181–93.

_____. "Yahweh's Generous Love: Eschatological Expectations in Hosea 14:2–9." *Old Testament Essays* 1 (1988): 27–48.

Lakoff, George. *Women, Fire, and Dangerous Things: What Categories Reveal about the Mind*. Chicago: University of Chicago Press, 2008.

_____. *Metaphors We Live By*. Chicago: University of Chicago Press, 2008.

Lakoff, George, and Zoltán Kövecses. "The Cognitive Model of Anger Inherent in American English." In *Cultural Models in Language and Thought*, 195–221. Ed. Dorothy Holland and Naomi Quinn. Cambridge: Cambridge University Press, 1987.

Lapsley, Jacqueline E. "Feeling Our Way: Love for God in Deuteronomy." *Catholic Biblical Quarterly* 65/3 (2003): 350–69.

Lazarus, Richard. *Emotion and Adaptation*. New York: Oxford University Press, 1994.

Lipiński, E. "שנא śāné'." *Theological Dictionary of the Old Testament*. 14 (1991): 164–74.

Lundbom, Jack R. *Jeremiah 1–20: A New Translation with Introduction and Commentary*. Garden City: Doubleday, 1999.

Lutz, Catherine. "The Domain of Emotion Words on Ifaluk." *American Ethnologist* 9 (1982): 113–28.

_____. *Unnatural Emotions: Everyday Sentiments on a Micronesian Atoll and Their Challenge to Western Theory*. Chicago: University of Chicago Press, 1988.

_____, and Geoffrey White, "Anthropology of Emotions." *Annual Review of Anthropology* 15 (1986): 405–36.

Macintosh, Andrew A. *Hosea: A Critical and Exegetical Commentary*. Edinburgh: T&T Clark, 1997.

Mallery, Paul, Suzanne Mallery, and Richard Gorsuch. "A Preliminary Taxonomy of Attributions to God." *International Journal for the Psychology of Religion* 10/3 (2000): 135–56.
Malul, Meir. "Adoption of Foundlings in the Bible and Mesopotamian Documents: A Study of Some Legal Metaphors in Ezekiel 16, 1–7." *Journal for the Study of the Old Testament* 46 (1990): 97–126.
Matthew, Michael. "Anger Management and Biblical Characters: A Study of 'Angry Exchange' among Characters of Hebrew Narratives." *Old Testament Abstracts* 29/2 (2015): 451–80.
Mathews, Kenneth. *Genesis 11:27–50:26*. Nashville: Broadman and Holman, 2005.
Matthews, Victor. "The Anthropology of Clothing within the Joseph Narrative." *Journal for the Study of the Old Testament* 20/65 (1995): 29–35.
McCarter, P. Kyle. *II Samuel: A New Translation with Introduction, Notes, and Commentary*. Garden City: Doubleday, 1984.
McKane, William A. *A Critical and Exegetical Commentary on Jeremiah*. Vol. 1. London: Bloomsbury Academic, 2000.
McKellar, Peter. "Provocation to Anger and the Development of Attitudes of Hostility." *British Journal of Psychology* 40/3 (1950): 104–14.
Melnyk, Janet. "When Israel Was a Child: Ancient Near Eastern Adoption Formulas and the Relationship between God and Israel." In *History and Interpretation: Essays in Honor of John H. Hayes*, 245–59. Ed. M. Patrick Graham, William P. Brown, and Jeffrey K. Kuan. Sheffield: Sheffield Academic Press, 1993.
Miller, Patrick. "Fire in the Mythology of Canaan and Israel." In *Israelite Religion and Biblical Theology: Collected Essays*. Sheffield: Sheffield Academic Press, 2000. 18–23.
Mirguet, Françoise. "What Is an 'Emotion' in the Hebrew Bible?" *Biblical Interpretation* 24 (2019): 442–64.
Moran, William L. "The Ancient Near Eastern Background of the Love of God in Deuteronomy." *Catholic Biblical Quarterly* 25/1 (1963): 77–87.
Nelson, Richard. *Deuteronomy: A Commentary*. Louisville: Westminster John Knox, 2004.
Nutkowitz, Hélène. "Concerning the Verb *Śn'* in Judaeo-Aramaic Contracts from Elephantine." *Journal of Semitic Studies* 52/2 (2007): 211–25.
Park, Jiyoung, and Shinobu Kitayama. "Anger Expression and Health: The Cultural Moderation Hypothesis." In *Oxford Handbook of Integrative Health Science*. Ed. Carol D. Ryff and Robert Kruger. New York: Oxford University Press, 2018. 379–93.
Plamper, Jan. *History of Emotions: An Introduction*. Oxford: Oxford University Press, 2017.
Propp, William. "Kinship in 2 Samuel 13." *Catholic Biblical Quarterly* 55 (1993): 39–53.
Redditt, Paul L. "The God Who Loves and Hates." In *Shall Not the Judge of All the Earth Do What Is Right? Studies on the Nature of God in Tribute to James Crenshaw*, 175–90. Ed. David Penchansky and Paul L. Redditt. Winona Lake: Eisenbrauns, 2000.
Rempel, John, Christopher Burris, and Darius Fathi. "Hate: Evidence for a Motivational Conceptualization." *Motivation and Emotion* 42 (2019): 179–90.

Riley, Andrew J. *Divine and Human Hate in the Ancient Near East: A Lexical Contextual Analysis.* Piscataway: Gorgias, 2017.
Rivera, Joseph de. *A Structural Theory of Emotion.* New York: International Universities Press, 1977.
Rofé, Alexander. "Defilement of Virgins in Biblical Law and the Case of Dinah (Genesis 34)." *Bib* 86 (2005): 369–75.
Rosch, Eleanor. "Cognitive Representations of Semantic Categories." *Journal of Experimental Psychology* 104 (1975): 192–235.
Royzman, Edward, Clark McCauley, and Paul Rozin "From Plato to Putnam: Four Ways to Think about Hate." In *The Psychology of Hate.* Ed. Robert Sternberg. Washington DC: American Psychological Association, 2005.
Rudman, Dominic. "Reliving the Rape of Tamar: Absalom's Revenge in 2 Samuel 13." *OTA* 1 (1998): 326–39.
Russell, James. "Culture and Categorization of Emotion." *Psychological Bulletin* 110 (1991): 426–50.
_____, and Beverly Fehr. "Fuzzy Concepts in a Fuzzy Hierarchy: Varieties of Anger." *Journal of Personality and Social Psychology* 67/2 (1994): 186–205.
Schlimm, Matthew. *From Fratricide to Forgiveness.* Winona Lake: Eisenbrauns, 2011.
Sharkin, Bruce S. "The Measurement and Treatment of Client Anger in Counseling." *Journal of Counseling and Development* 66/8 (1988): 361–5.
Shaver, Phillip, et al. "Emotion Knowledge: Further Exploration of a Prototype Approach." *Journal of Personality and Social Psychology* 52/6 (1987): 1061–86.
Siebert-Hommes, Jopie. "'With Bands of Love': Hosea 11 as 'Recapitulation of the Basic Themes of the Book of Hosea.'" In *Unless Some One Guide Me: Festchrift for Karel A. Deurloo.* Ed. J. W. Dyk et al. Maastricht: Shaker, 2001.
Simian-Yofre, Besel H., and Heinz-Josef Fabry. "נחם *Nḥm.*" *Theological Dictionary of the Old Testament* 9 (1998): 340–55.
Simkovich, Malka. "Esau the Ancestor of Rome." Thetorah.com
Slabbert, Martin J. "Coping in a Harsh Reality: The Concept of the 'Enemy' in the Composition of Psalms 9 and 10." *HTS Theological Studies* 71/3 (2015): 1–5.
Smith, Craig, and Phoebe Ellsworth. "Patterns of Cognitive Appraisal in Emotion." *Journal of Personality and Social Psychology* 48/4 (1985): 813–38.
Solomon, Robert C. *True to Our Feelings: What Our Emotions Are Really Telling Us.* New York: Oxford, 2008.
Spronk, Klaas. *Historical Commentary of the Old Testament: Judges.* Leuven: Peeters, 2019.
Sternberg, Robert J. *The Psychology of Hate.* Washington, DC: American Psychological Association, 2005.
Swanepoel, M. G. "Ezekiel 16: Abandoned Child, Bride Adorned or Unfaithful Wife?" In *Among the Prophets: Language, Imagery and Structure in the Prophetic Writings.* Ed. Philip Davies and David Clines. Sheffield: Sheffield Academic Press, 1993.
Sweeney, Marvin. *The Prophetic Literature.* Nashville: Abingdon, 2005.
_____. *The Twelve Prophets.* 2 vols. Berit Olam. Collegeville: Liturgical Press, 2000.

Bibliography 101

Szubin, Zvi Henry, and Bezalel Porten. "The Status of the Repudiated Spouse: A New Interpretation of Kraeling," *Israel Law Review* 35/1 (2002): 46–78.

Trible, Phyllis. *Texts of Terror: Literary-Feminist Readings of Biblical Narratives.* Minneapolis: Fortress, 1984.

Tsumura, David Toshio. *The Second Book of Samuel.* Grand Rapids: Eerdmans, 2019.

———. *The First Book of Samuel.* Grand Rapids: Eerdmans, 2007.

VanGemeren, Willem A. Ed. *New International Dictionary of the Old Testament Theology and Exegesis.* Vol. 3. Grand Rapids: Zondervan, 1997.

Wagner, Andreas. *Haas: Emotionen Gefühle und Sprache Im Alten Testament: Vier Studien.* Waltrop: Hartmut Spenner, 2006.

Wagner, S. "מאס *Mā,as.*" *Theological Dictionary of the Old Testament* 8: 49–59.

Wallis, Gerhard, Jan Bergman, and A. O. Haldar. "אהב *'āhabh.*" *Theological Dictionary of the Old Testament* 1: 104–12.

Waltke, Bruce. "Cain and His Offering." *Westminster Theological Journal* 48/2 (1986): 212–30.

Wells, Bruce. "The Hated Wife in Deuteronomic Law." *VT* 60/1 (2010): 131–46.

Wenham, Gordon. *Genesis 16–50.* Nashville: Thomas Nelson, 1994.

Westermann, Claus. *Genesis 1–11: A Continental Commentary.* Transl. John Scullion. Minneapolis MN.: Fortress, 1990.

———. John Scullion. Ed. *Genesis 37–50: A Continental Commentary.* Minneapolis: Augsburg, 1986.

———, and John Scullion. Ed. *Genesis 12–36: A Continental Commentary.* Minneapolis: Augsburg Fortress, 1985.

Wierzbicka, Anna. *Emotions across Languages and Cultures: Diversity and Universals.* Cambridge: Cambridge University Press, 1999.

———. *Semantics, Culture, and Cognition: Universal Human Concepts in Culture-Specific Configurations.* New York: Oxford University Press, 1992.

———. "Human Emotions: Universal or Culture-Specific," *American Anthropologist* 88 (1986): 584–94.

Wildberger, Hans. *Isaiah 1–12.* Minneapolis: Fortress, 1991.

van Wolde, Ellen. *Reframing Biblical Studies: When Language and Text Meet Culture, Cognition, and Context.* Winona Lake: Eisenbrauns, 2009.

Wolff, Hans Walter. *Hosea: A Commentary on the Book of the Prophet Hosea.* Minneapolis: Fortress, 1974.

Wyatt, Nicholas. "The Story of Dinah and Shechem." *UF* 22 (1990): 433–58.

Index

NOTE: Page numbers in bold refer to tables and those followed by "n" refer to notes.

Ammonites 38
Amos: Amos 5 59n14; Amos 5:21 60n27; Amos 5:21–24 52; Amos 5:26–27 52; Amos 6:8–9 51
anger: biblical 62, 67n17; cognitive antecedents 19–20, 25n31; control of 20, 25n36; as fires of war 84; hate inhibited in 22–23, 26n43; as human army 83–84; as a liquid 85; in marital relationships 17, 45n27; modern English anger 26n39; prototype studies 19–20; reported responses 20; against unfair or unjust treatment 20, 25n32
anger-scripts 5, 12n21; Chinese *nu* 6; cultural differences 6; gender differences 27n44; metaphors and metonymies 5–6, 20–22, **21**, 26n37, 83–85
avoidance 22, 50

Baloian, Bruce 62
biblical emotions 7–10; ancient Israelite concepts 7; anger 62, 67n17; association of haters with enemies 32n8; *sn'* and *ḥrh* concepts 8–10; *vs* modern English terms 8; *see also ḥrh*-script; *sn'*-script
blameworthiness 19–20, 23n4, 25n33
Branson, Robert 29
Brice, Gene 29
Briggs, Jean 91–92
Broad-Biblical *ḥrh*-script 63, **63**, **93**; biblical metaphors and metonymies 64–65; cause of biblical anger 63–64; descriptions of divine *ḥrh* 64; human beings as containers 64–65, 66n12; portrayals of God 65
Broad-Biblical *sn'*-script 30–31, 32n8, 33, 51–52; God's likenesses and God's differences 51–52; God's reaction 52; vulnerability of God 52
Burris, Christopher 16, 18

Canadian Inuits 91
cognition 2
cognitive linguistics 91
cross-cultural emotion differences 2–3

Daniel 3 72–74; Dan 3:13 73; Dan 3:15 74; Dan 3:16–18 74; Dan 3:19 74; Dan 3:28 74
Darwin, Charles 1
Davitz, J. R. 16
Deuteronomy 57; Deut 1:27 60n21, 60n27; Deut 2:12 59n17; Deut 6:5 93; Deut 9:9–10 49; Deut 9:25–29 54; Deut 9:28 60n27; Deut 12:31 60n20, 60n27; Deut 16:22 55; Deut 21:15–17 29, 40, 43–44; Deut 22:13–15 43–44; Deut 22:28 78n4; Deut 22:28–29 42; Deut 22:33–27 79n14; Deut 24:1–4 58, 61n29; Deut 24:3 43–44; Deut 25:3 79n24; Deut 32:41 48, 58n3; Deut 33:11 48, 58n3; spousal *sn'* in 58
Divine *ḥrh*-script: context of war and death 85; God as divine warrior 81–83; God's *'p/ḥmh/qṣp* 84; old poetic and prophetic variants 81; Synergistic Warrior *Ḥrh*-Script 83–85

Divine Kinsman Ḥrh-Script 86–87
Divine sn'-script 50–51, 53–57; body parts 56–57; God's sn' for Esau 54–55; hating of objects 55–56; Israel's accusation of God 55, 60n21; justness of God's sn' 55–57; Moses' warnings 55; targeting of guilty 53–55; use of metonymy 55, 60n22
divorce 57–58

Eidevall, Göran 52
Ekman, Paul 1, 3
emotion knowledge 25n34
emotions 52; biblical terms 7–10; of common conceptual category 4, 12n18; conceptual category BACHELOR 4; cross-cultural differences 2–3; Darwin's view 1; emotional lexicons of different languages 2; facial expressions 1; individual differences 1–3; mental representation 3; as physiological changes 1, 10n1; prototypes 3–4; as social constructions 2; traits essential to 3, 11n13; universal 1, 3, 8, 10, 11n2
emotion-scripts 4–5; anger-script 5–6; hate-script 5; Japanese *on* concept 5; shame 5; variants 6–7
English hate-script, modern 19
English lexicon 2
Esther: Esth 1:16–22 75; Esth 1:18 66n11; Esth 2:1–4 75; Esth 2:21 66n11; Esth 3 72–73; Esth 3:1–7 72; Esth 3:12–15 73; Esth 7 78n1
Evil-Targeted sn'-script 47, 49–50
Exodus: Exod 15:3–8 82; Exod 15:7 82; Exod 15:7, 17 66n10; Exod 15:10 83; Exod 15:18 82–83; Exod 23:5 44
Ezekiel: Ezek 20:8 66n10; Ezek 25:13–15 88n8

Fathi, Darius 16, 18
Fehr, Beverly 6
Fitness, Julie 17–19, 22–23
Fletcher, Garth 17–19, 22

Genesis: Gen 4 77–78, 80n30; Gen 4:5–11 77; Gen 4:13–14 78; Gen 24:16 58n3; Gen 26:12–13 37; Gen 26:27–29 38; Gen 27 78n1; Gen 29:13–28 39; Gen 29:18, 20 40; Gen 29:23–35 39; Gen 29:28–30 40; Gen 29:32 40; Gen 30 76; Gen 30:1 76; Gen 30:2 76; Gen 31:35 80n27; Gen 34:2 69; Gen 34:7 70, 78n5, 80n32; Gen 34:9 70; Gen 34:25–29 70; Gen 34:31 70; Gen 36:1 59n17; Gen 37:2–5 35–36; Gen 37:4 43; Gen 37:12 35; Gen 37:14 35; Gen 37:19 35; Gen 37:20–23 36; Gen 37:25–28 38; Gen 37:26–27 36; Gen 37:34–35 36; Gen 39:3 72; Gen 39:4 71; Gen 39:4–6 71; Gen 39:14, 17 71; Gen 39:17–18 71; Gen 42–45 36; Gen 44:18 36; Gen 45:9–11 36; Gen 49:5–7 79n12; Gen 39:19b–20 71
God 31, 47, 64–65, 73–74, 81; anger of 85; cup of ḥmh 85; in Deuteronomy 60n20; as divine warrior 81–83; dominance over haters 48–49, 58n3; enemies of 32n8; harming of targets 51–52; ḥrh 70; Israel's acknowledgment of 86–87, 89n21, 90n25; likenesses and differences 51–52; 'p/ḥmh/ qṣp 84; reactions 52; reputation of 55; restraint of ḥrh 86, 90n24; righteous anger 62; rod of 'ap/z'm 84; and social injustice 49–50, 55–56, 59n14; sovereignty 49; s sn' for Esau 54–55; targeting of guilty 53–55; temperance 10, 87; vulnerability of 52
God-Targeted sn'-Script 10, 47–49; Divine sn'-script; portrayal of God harming haters 48–49, 58n3; *see also* Broad-Biblical sn'-script
gren jai 2

hate 57–58; causes of 17; definition 14–15, 24n11; hostile attitudes 15–16; humiliation and 19; impulse to harm 15–18; inhibited in anger 22–23, 26n43; lasting hostility 23; in marital relationships 17, 45n27; nihilistic 17–18; primary function of 60n20; prototype studies 15–22; retributive 17; statements 24n19; urge to avoid 18; urge to "physically hurt the partner" 17, 24n22
hate-scripts 5; modern English 19
Heine, Bernd 56

104 Index

Hivites 70
Hosea: Hos 9:15 60n27; Hos 9:15-17 51; Hos 11 86–87
ḥrh-script 8–10, 13n28, 23; portrayal of God 10; see also Broad-Biblical ḥrh-script; Divine ḥrh-script
Hugenberger, Gordon 57
humiliation 19, 22

illegitimate worship 56
impulse to harm 15–18
Isaiah: Isa 1:11–15 52, 59n12; Isa 1:14 60n27; Isa 5:24 88n6; Isa 5:25–30 88n8; Isa 9:7–10:4 88n8; Isa 13:3–6 88n8; Isa 33:11 88n6; Isa 40:24 88n6; Isa 47:14 88n6; Isa 51:19–22 85; Isa 61:8 56, 60n27, 61n33

Jeremiah: Jer 10:10, 24–25 66n10; Jer 12:7–8 52; Jer 12:8 60n27; Jer 13:24 88n6; Jer 21:5–7 84, 88n8; Jer 21:5–14 84; Jer 21:10–14 84; Jer 21:13–14 84; Jer 25:15–16 85; Jer 25:27–28 85; Jer 44:4 60n20, 60n24; Jer 50:25 88n8
Job 8:22 58n3, 59n4
Job 41:20 88n6
Joel 2:5 88n6
Joshua: Josh 7 71; Josh 7:5–11 70; Josh 7:24–26 70
Judges: Judg 11:1–11 36–38; Judg 14:12–15 39–40; Judg 14–15 78n1

kin-targeted ḥrh-scripts 68, 74–78; Abel's offering over Cain's 77–78; Ahasuerus's ḥrh at Vashti 75–76; Jacob's ḥrh at Rachel 76; between Jonathan and Saul 74–75
Kövecses, Zoltán 5, 22, 26n39, 65, 66n12

Lakoff, George 5, 22, 65
Lazarus, Richard 1, 11n4, 19–20
lexeme 29, 31n3
love 54
Lutz, Catherine 2

Malachi 59n17; Mal 1:2 54; Mal 1:3 51, 60n27; Mal 1:16 58; Mal 2:16 57, 60n27; Mal 3:13 88n6
male-targeted sn'-script 33–38; Joseph's brothers (Genesis 37, 45) 34–36; sympathy towards hater 33–34
marital relationships, emotions in 17–19, 27n45; responses for hate and anger in 17, 27n45, 43–44
Mathews, Kenneth 36
McKellar, Peter 15–16
Mirguet, Françoise 8

narrative ḥrh-scripts: authority in 68–69; kin-targeted 68, 74–78; outsider-targeted 68–74
narrative sn'-scripts 45n1; Amnon and Tamar 41–43; emotional desperation 39–41; irrevocability of consequences 41–43; Jephthah's brothers/Gileadites 36–38, 52; Joseph's brothers 34–36; Laban's deceit to Jacob's sn' 39–41; Philistines and Samson 39–41; spousal sn' 39–41
Nelson, Richard 55
nihilistic hate 17–18
Numbers: Num 10:35 48, 58n3; Num 20:14–21 59n17

Obadiah 1:18 88n6
outsider-targeted ḥrh-scripts 68–74; account of Haman's ḥmh and Nebuchadnezzar's ḥmh 72–74; between Dinah and Shechem 69–70

powerlessness 23
prototypes 3–4
Proverbs 56–57; Prov 6 56; Prov 6:16 60n27; Prov 6:16–19 61n33; Prov 11 28
Psalms: Ps 2:5–6 66n10; Ps 5:5–7 53; Ps 5:6 59n6, 60n27; Ps 9:13 49; Ps 11 28–29; Ps 11:5 53, 59n6, 60n27; Ps 11:6 51; Ps 18:17–18, 40–41 49; Ps 18:41 58n3; Ps 21:9–12 48; Ps 25:19 48–49; Ps 26:4–5 50; Ps 26:4–9 50; Ps 26:5 59n6; Ps 31:7 59n6; Ps 34:21 59n4; Ps 35:19 48; Ps 36:3 59n6; Ps 38:19 48; Ps 41:8 49; Ps 44:6–8 49; Ps 45:8 50, 59n6; Ps 50:17 59n4; Ps 55:13 49; Ps 68:1 48; Ps 69:5 48–49; Ps 81:6 58n3; Ps 81:16 58n3; Ps 83:13 88n6; Ps 86:17 58n3; Ps 97:10 59n5; Ps 101:1–3 59n6; Ps 101:3 50, 59n6; Ps 118:7 58n3; Ps 119:13 50; Ps

119:104, 113, 128, 163 59n6; Ps 119:127–28 50

Rempel, John 16, 18
retributive hate 17
Riley, Andrew 29, 44, 55, 60n20
Rudman, Dominic 42
Russell, James 6, 47

1 Samuel 1:6 66n11
1 Samuel 17 78n1
1 Samuel 20: 1 Sam 15:28 75; 1 Sam 20:30–33 74–75
2 Samuel 1:23 75
2 Samuel 13 41–43, 78n1; 2 Sam 13:1–2 42; 2 Sam 13:14–17 41–42; 2 Sam 13:19–22 42; 2 Sam 13:28 43; 2 Samuel 13:21 79n22
2 Samuel 22:18 47, 58n3
2 Samuel 22:41 58n3
Schlimm, Matthew 63, 70, 78n8
sn'-script 8–10, 23; affective and non-emotive traits associated with 29–30, 32n8; in biblical narratives 30–31, 32n8, 33; definitions 29; Divine 50–51, 53–57; Evil-Targeted 47, 49–50; female-targeted 33–34, 38–43; in Gen 29:30 28–29; God-Targeted 47–49; history of 28–30; idealized model of 30; legal 43–44; literal sense 29; male-targeted 33–38; prototype approach 30; sequence of traits 30–31; social standing 34
social justice and social injustice 50, 53
Synergistic Warrior *Ḥrh*-Script 83–85

Tsumura, David 42

urge to avoid 18
Utku community 91–92

van Wolde, Ellen 63, 65

Westermann, Claus 35
Wierzbicka, Anna 2–3, 8

Zechariah: Zech 8:17 56, 60n27, 61n33
Zephaniah 3:8–9 66n10